In Their Shoes

Edited by Yolanda Fernandez, Ph.D.

Published by:

Wood 'N' Barnes Publishing & Distribution
Oklahoma City, Oklahoma 73112
405-942-6812

Cover Art by Blue Designs
Copyediting & Design by Ramona Cunningham

Printed in the United States of America
Oklahoma City, Oklahoma
ISBN # 1-885473-48-6

CONTENTS

This book is dedicated to
my husband and son, Gord and Nicholas,
and to the many clients I have worked with over the years who
made me a better, and more empathic, therapist.

Introduction

My interest in empathy began in 1992 soon after I began working with my supervisor (and now colleague) Dr. Bill Marshall. At that time we were running a sexual offender treatment program in a minimum-security federal penitentiary. Our treatment program, like most others, included an empathy enhancing component. At the time there appeared to be a consensus among treatment providers that sexual offenders must suffer from an empathy deficit. It made intuitive sense that a deficit in empathy would allow these men to commit the offenses against their victims. Unfortunately, however, there was little research to support this conclusion. As a young and enthusiastic researcher I concluded that this was an "empirical question" and I chose to examine empathy deficits in sexual offenders as my undergraduate thesis. I have been fascinated by the topic ever since.

Dr. Marshall suggested that I begin my research by reviewing and creating an overview of the established literature on empathy. This task was easier said than done. As will become apparent in this book the literature lacks a concise definition or approach to measuring empathy and little has changed in the last 10 years. The ambiguity in the empathy literature makes it a difficult concept to understand and study. Yet, philosophers, researchers, and clinicians all agree that empathy is a crucial skill to effective human interactions. In addition, despite the lack of a clear definition of empathy there is some evidence that empathy can be identified in others and taught as a skill.

When I was first asked to edit a book on empathy I was interested but wary of the project. Despite having thoroughly reviewed the literature on empathy and completed a number of my own studies on empathy in sexual offenders, I still felt as though I had a tenuous grasp on empathy as a concept. I eventually decided that editing this book would force me to create a clearer framework of empathy and, as a consequence, illuminate my understanding. In my opinion, this was accomplished through the contributions of the various authors who have done an excellent job of making sense of this confusing literature. Having now completed the book I feel that I do, indeed, have a better personal understanding of empathy, although part of that understanding has been an acceptance that empathy, in many ways, remains an indistinct concept and our ability to measure it is questionable at best. I believe the chapters in this book will also provide readers with an improved understanding of empathy, but more importantly, I hope it spurs readers toward creating more concise definitions, improved measures, and better research on empathy.

Yolanda Fernandez

Historical Foundations & Current Conceptualizations of Empathy

W.L. Marshall

"Faith in the creative process, in the dynamics of emergence,
in the values and purposes that transcend past achievements and past forms,
is the precondition of all further growth." Lewis Mumford (1895-1990)

The study of empathic processes has been applied to a wide range of human and animal behaviors. Among humans, empathy has been employed to explain or illuminate aspects of friendship (Colvin, Voight, & Ickes, 1997), intimate relationships (Brehm, 1992), marital issues (Sillars & Scott, 1983), moral development (Blum, 1980), art appreciation (Wind, 1963), altruism (Batson, 1987), aggression (Miller & Eisenberg, 1988), group survival (Plutchik, 1987), personality judgements (Asch, 1946; McCrae, 1982), and changes induced by psychological treatment (Katz, 1963; Kohut, 1959; Rogers, 1959) to name a few of the areas that have used the concept persistently. A reader might think from this that there was an agreed upon definition of empathy and a corresponding measure that all were using. This reader would be quite wrong. Almost every study of empathy employs a different concept; although, these different definitions often share some features. The measures that are available differ significantly, and there are questions about their psychometric properties (Chlopan, McCain, Carbonell, & Hagen, 1985).

In this chapter, an attempt will be made to trace the history of the concept and outline some of the most important issues concerning its conceptualization. We hope this will give the interested reader some appreciation for the confusion in the field and hopefully some reasonable clarity by the end of the chapter about what is meant by the term "empathy" and how it is generated.

In his classic text, *The expression of the emotions in man and animals*, Charles Darwin (1873) makes it clear that he believed there was empathic communication between humans and between humans and other animals and that other animals displayed affective communication with each other. Darwin noted that his pet dog responded accurately to his emotions. When Darwin was delighted with some news, his dog would respond with apparent joy; when he was gloomy, his dog would not only appear sad, but it would also attempt to comfort Darwin. These responses of animals to human emotions are, of course, familiar to all pet owners, but few owners recognize, as Darwin did, that this emotional communication is also evident between animals. One day while I was walking two dogs who had not met each other before, one of them (Louie), who was obviously more timid than the other (Duster), became stranded on a rocky ledge. All of Louie's attempts to get down and my attempts to assist him failed. While we were making these efforts, Duster appeared anxious and he kept crying out in seeming distress and it was clear that this was aimed at Louie. Finally Duster despaired of our attempts and ran some distance around the cliff until he was beside Louie. Duster then came forward to my arms with Louie at his side, and I was able to rescue Louie. It was very clear to me that Duster displayed distress at Louie's predicament and acted to end Louie's misfortune. Studies of social deprivation among animals show that it results in serious deficits in social competence including a lack of empathy (Ginsburg, 1991).

From the earliest writings on empathy between people, it has been suggested that this capacity to recognize and respond to other people's distress is evident from the very earliest days of people's lives. More recently, a considerable amount of research has focused on this display of empathy among children (Ainsworth, 1973; Eisenberg, Murphy, & Shepard, 1997; Feshbach, 1978). When my grandson, Patrick, was three years old, he received a tricycle for his birthday and took it to daycare to show it off. Shortly before lunch at the daycare, one of the little girls fell and hurt herself while playing. She began to cry and was obviously distraught. Patrick got off his tricycle, went directly to her, put his arm around her shoulder and told her not to cry. "You can ride my bike," Patrick said to her in a clear attempt to comfort the girl. Clearly this is a display of empathy/sympathy at an early age. But not all children show empathy when faced with another's suffering; some attempt to escape, while others respond with anger or anxiety (Eisenberg & Miller, 1987). Adults sometimes blame the victims of misfortune (Shaver, 1970). Empathy then may not be universal among humans, or it may not be a trait that is consistently displayed (Cottrell, 1942; Mischel, 1968). Despite Darwin's somewhat anthropomorphizing tendency in the passages of his brilliant book (and perhaps my own in the above illustration), it is clear he considered these empathic processes critical to the creation and maintenance of social order among many, if not most, mammalian species.

Darwin was not the first serious writer, however, to identify empathy as an important social process. The first person to use the term "sympathy" to explain aspects of human behavior appears to have been the Scottish empiricist philosopher, David Hume (1711-1776). Hume introduced the term in his book on moral development (Hume, 1739), and later Adam Smith (1723-1790), another Scottish philosopher and economist, similarly claimed a crucial role for sympathy in moral motivations (Smith, 1759). Both social theorists thought sympathy was necessary to understand how people could know the feelings of others and thereby act compassionately. Baldwin, an early American psychologist, captured this notion when he wrote that in sympathy, "the external and indeed internal boundaries between you and me are swept away, and I feel your calamity really as my own" (Baldwin, 1897, p. 224).

It appears to have been in analysis of the asthetic experience (i.e., how we appreciate art in all its forms) that the notion of empathy was first given expression. Aristotle (384-322 BC), in discussing art, metaphysics, and psychology (e.g., in *Poetics*, *De Anima*, *Rhetoric*, and *Metaphysics*), was concerned to understand the processes by which poetry, drama, music, and painting could evoke such strong emotional responses. He concluded that these emotional attributes were evoked by the viewer or listener in response to features inherent (although not obviously so) in the work itself (Copleston, 1985; Durant, 1961). Art, Aristole said, appeals to both intellect and feelings, a remark that presages modern views of empathy as having both cognitive and emotional components. Later writers on asthetics explicitly used the term "empathy" to describe "the projection of human feelings, emotions, and attitudes into inanimate objects (i.e., works of art)" (Gilbert & Kuhn, 1939, p. 42, section in parentheses added). In fact, empathy was used as an explanatory concept predominantly in the field of asthetics before it entered the broader domains of psychology (Gilbert & Kuhn, 1939; Hunsdahl, 1967; Listowel, 1933), and it was in the analysis of the asthetic empathic process that research on empathy was first initiated (Lee & Anstruther-Thompson, 1912).

German scholars of the nineteenth century became interested in what they called "einfuhlung" (Rader, 1935), which was later translated by Edward Titchener (1909) into English as "empathy." The interests of these German scholars, however, was still primarily within asthetics. Their approach to this study of how we appreciate art was, however, primarily philosophical speculation or logical analysis of the term "empathy." With the remarkable advances in and successes of experimental empiricism applied to psychological phenomena (e.g., as evident in the work of Fechner, Helmholtz, and Wundt), there was a shift in emphasis to the "new scientific methods" (Gladstein, 1984). Unfortunately, this enthusiastic application of empirical methods did not initially involve a focus on empathy, but it did bring about a shift away from "armchair" speculation.

One of the major writers on asthetic empathy, Theodor Lipps (1903), extended his notion of empathy to a consideration of how individuals recognize and respond to other people's thoughts and feelings (Lipps, 1913). He was not, unfortunately, at all interested in what this response prompted people to do. He had no interest in sympathy or in attempts to ameliorate the distress of others. Nevertheless, the roots of much of the later works on empathy lie in the works of the nineteenth century German scholars, and Lipps was pre-eminent among them. Lipps, in fact, believed that we all inherit a faculty that generates empathy, a notion that reappears much later in modern research (Buck & Ginsberg, 1997; Hoffman, 1981).

The two streams evident in the literature reviewed to this point focused on either sympathy or empathy, with neither stream seeming to have much contact with the other. In fact, the distinction between the meaning of these two terms was remarked upon by Lipps (1913) and by Scheler (1913). Scheler used the term "sympathy" to describe the recognition of emotions in others and the compassionate response it triggers, whereas Lipps was more interested, as we have learned, in the emotional responses prompted by either art or another's display of emotions.

The American sociologist Charles Cooley (1902) wrote expansively on sympathy, which he said was the sharing of another person's mental or emotional state without the pity implicit in the everyday use of this term. In Cooley's view, then, sympathy was essentially identical to what the earlier German writers had called "empathy." George Mead, another American sociologist, disagreed with Cooley by suggesting that sympathy was what led people to assist others (Mead, 1934). Sympathy, Mead said, involves "the arousing in one's self of the attitude of the individual whom one is assisting ... We feel with him and we are able so to feel ourselves into the other" (Mead, 1934, p.299). To this, he added "sympathy... springs from (the) ... capacity to take the role of the other person" (Mead, 1934, p.366). For Mead, then, sympathy involved the ability to recognize attitudes and emotions in others, to adopt the perspective of others, and take actions to reduce the distress of others. This is very close to modern notions of empathy. In fact, Mead's work on sympathy was crucial to the shift away from the philosophic focus on asthetic empathy to more scientifically-based research. His distinction between empathy and sympathy lives on with current scholars still struggling with the distinction between these concepts and with their relationship to each other (e.g., Aronfreed, 1970; Hanson, 1997).

McDougall (1908) in his *Introduction to Social Psychology*, described sympathy as "the experiencing of any feeling or emotion...we observe in other persons" (p. 92). McDougall did not, however, limit his notion to simply responses to the suffering of others. He saw the contagious effects of laughter as "the most familiar example of sympathetic induction of an affective state" (McDougall, 1908, p.94). Clearly, McDougall saw emotional responding as the key component of the sympathetic response. Allport (1924) thought that sympathy facilitated a greater understanding in human relationships and was dependent upon the person's own emotional history (or habits, as he put it) rather than resulting from instinctual responses as had been claimed by McDougall. This was the first theory to explicitly declare that sympathy (or empathy) was a learned experience; although, Lee and Anstruther-Thompson (1912) held similar views. Obviously, if empathy (or sympathy) is learned, then it can be taught, which, of course, is a necessary assumption in all programs involving empathy training.

The great developmental psychologist, Jean Piaget (1929), described what he called "decentering," which is a process that involves both cognitive and emotional responses. This process is the basis for the emergence of a recognition of others as being distinct from the self. He considered these two processes inseparable and felt they clearly functioned as one. Unlike Allport, Piaget believed that tendencies to be sympathic were present in the earliest stages of life and that these were "the raw material of all subsequent moral behavior" (Piaget, 1932, p. 398). It was through the process of emerging decentering that the child is able to direct these sympathetic reactions toward others. Piaget's writings formed the basis for the views of empathy of subsequent developmental psychologists, and this became an important area of research. This research into the developmental features of sympathy or empathy has, as we will see later in this book (Chapter 3), informed the whole field of empathy research.

In the social psychology literature, Cottrell (1942) appears to have been the first to use the term empathy to describe the "process of responding by reproducing the acts of the other" (p. 374). Cottrell called for a new approach to these phenomena declaring that the established "trait" approach was inadequate to the understanding of interpersonal behavior. The trait approach to empathy suggests that whatever empathic capacity a person has will be shown in all, or almost all, situations. That is, it is a feature of each person that is either present or not, regardless of the circumstances. What was needed, Cottrell said, was "a situational frame of reference" and an attempt by the researcher to develop the skills necessary to "assimilate himself to...the perspective of his subject" (p. 381). This led to the development of research paradigm employed in a series of studies (Cottrell & Dymond, 1949) whose findings supported Cottrell's situationalist view of empathy.

Psychotherapy writings have, since the time of Freud, stressed the role of empathy in both understanding and changing the behavior of clients. Freud (1922) thought empathy was the major way in which we understand other people, particularly those whose experiences and beliefs are different from our own. Sullivan (1947) took up Freud's ideas, and in his interpersonal theory of personality development, empathy played a vital role. Since Sullivan thought that the basic issue in life was learning to cope with anxiety, he had to account for from where this anxiety arose. He believed it arose from the fact that tension in the mother induced anxiety in the infant; through an empathic process. Thus, for Sullivan empathy was the result of emotional contagion.

Theodore Reik, on the other hand, focused more on the role of empathy in the therapeutic process. He saw empathy as an unconscious interaction between the therapist and client. The client, Reik said, "is taken into your (i.e., the therapist's) ego and becomes, for the time being, a part of your ego" (Reik, 1948, p. 234, section in parentheses added). In developing these ideas further, Stewart (1956) declared empathy the deliberate attempt to identify with another person. For Stewart it was "both a process of intuition and the basis for dynamic inference" (p. 12). Empathy, in Stewart's view, was the way the therapist came to understand the client and was a skill critical to effective therapy. Kohut (1978) has more recently construed empathy as crucial both in psychoanalysis and in the understanding of others that is so essential to human relationships. Kohut, in fact, has generated the most comprehensive theories about the role of empathy in assisting clients to discover themselves and to free themselves from narcissism.

However, the most influential therapist, in terms of giving empathy a central role in treatment, was without a doubt Carl Rogers. In his landmark paper *Significant Aspects of Client-Centered Therapy*, Rogers (1942) suggested that a "deep understanding" of the client was one of the necessary conditions of effective therapy.

This involved an understanding and acceptance of the client's "emotionalized attitudes" and an attempt to understand the client's view of him/herself. In his later book, *Client-Centered Therapy*, he speaks of the therapist's "empathic attitude" where the therapist should "assume, in so far as he is able, the internal frame of reference of the client, to perceive the world as the client sees it, to perceive the client as he is seen by himself...and to communicate ... this empathic understanding to the client" (Rogers, 1951, p.29). In this quote, it is clear that Rogers saw that it was not only necessary for the therapist to attempt to accurately perceive and feel the emotional and attitudinal state of his clients, it was also essential to let them know that he understood their feeling and views.

The very clear views of Rogers that empathy is a necessary condition of effective therapy became the basis for an extensive body of research that has over the years confirmed his views (see the recent review by Marshall et al; in press). Rogers thought that empathy, along with genuineness and warmth, were the necessary and sufficient conditions for effective therapy. Research has suggested that empathy may be necessary to maximize treatment benefits but is not a sufficient condition to produce change.

Contentious Issues

Trait/State Views of Empathy

We have already noted Cottrell's (1942) concern with the trait approach of his time. As we have seen, when empathy is viewed as a trait, it is conceptualized as a disposition toward being empathic, that is evident in most, if not all, situations and is directed toward most, if not all, people. Cottrell challenged this view claiming that situational features determined the nature of the empathic response. This situational view had little influence at the time but was revived by Walter Mischel (1968) who wrote what has become the classic attack on trait approaches to personality. However, the prevalent view in empathy research to this day is to treat it as a trait, and almost all current measures are based on this assumption. Trait perspectives of empathy rest on evidence showing that people display cross-person consistency in empathy (Marangoni, Garcia, Ickes & Teng, 1995); although, the evidence is not extensive.

It seems evident from everyday experience that people are not consistently empathic toward all who are distressed. Few people felt empathy or sympathy for Herman Goering as he sat weeping in the defendant's seat at the Nuremberg War Crime Trials after World War II, and yet Goering was obviously distressed. Indeed, dramatists, novelists, and movie-makers would be markedly limited if they were unable to manipulate their audiences' empathic responses. Skilled writers can evoke empathy in their readers to even the vilest character. Not surprisingly, there is extensive evidence indicating that a variety of situational (Batson, 1987; Fultz, Schaller, & Cialdini, 1988; Strayer, 1993) and personal features (Davis & Kraus, 1997; Thomas & Fletcher, 1997) moderate empathic responding. Recently some researchers working with sexual offenders have abandoned trait measures of empathy, partly because the literature appears to suggest these men do not lack empathy toward all people (Marshall & Maric, 1996; Rapaport & Burkhart, 1984; Seto, 1992). These researchers (Beckett & Fisher, 1994; Fernandez & Marshall, in press; Fernandez, Marshall, Lightbody, & O'Sullivan, 1999; Hanson & Scott, 1995; McGrath, Cann, & Konopasky, 1998) have developed victim-specific measures, and these have proved very useful in work with sexual offenders. It seems likely the same will be true for other men who assault people.

Empathy/Sympathy Distinction

Throughout the history of the use of these terms, they have consistently been confused. Some writers use sympathy to mean the same as what others mean by empathy (Dymond, 1949; Feshbach, 1975), while some others use the terms interchangeably (Feshbach, 1978; Hogan, 1969; Ohbuchi, 1988). Still other writers have made very clear distinctions between the two terms (Miller & Eisenberg, 1988; Wispe, 1986). Wispe (1986), for example, identifies empathy as an attempt to understand the experience of another person; whereas, she sees sympathy as the direct perceptual awareness of another's experience. Wispe's definition of sympathy is very similar to what has been called "emotional contagion," a response best illustrated by the infectious nature of laughter but also evident in the sadness evoked in observers by another person's response to a tragic loss (Hodges & Wegner, 1997). These failures to clearly distinguish empathy and sympathy have been noted by numerous authors (Gladstein, 1984; Hickson, 1985; Levenson & Ruef, 1992).

Eisenberg (2000) says sympathy is a response that may be induced by empathy, and it involves feelings of sorrow and concern for someone who is upset. Empathy, she says, is an emotional response to another's state that is a match, or nearly so, with the other person's emotion. As Eisenberg points out, empathy does not necessarily lead to a sympathetic response. Capturing this idea in a schematic outline of the process, Batson, Fultz, and Schoenrade (1987) note that observing another person's discomfort may, under some conditions, generate such excessive personal distress in the viewer that he/she may become entirely self-focused. When these distressing responses occur, Batson et al. note, the viewer may be motivated to reduce his/her own distress rather than generate a sympathetic response. Consistent with Batson et al.'s idea, Hanson (1997) says empathy will lead to sympathy (i.e., a response meant to ameliorate the other person's distress) only if three preconditions are met: empathy is accurate, there exists a caring or benign relationship between the observer and the observed, and the observer has the ability to cope with the distress induced in them. These notions are based on a substantial body of literature, and they sit well with the idea that empathy is largely situationally determined.

RECENT CONCEPTUALIZATIONS

Aside from the confusion over the distinction between empathy and sympathy, the term empathy itself has generated a plethora of definitions, most of which have at least some aspects in common. Although some earlier writers (Feshbach, 1978; Hogan, 1969; Mehrabian, & Epstein, 1972; Stotland, 1969) argued about whether empathy is strictly a cognitive process (e.g., recognition of another's emotional state, ability to take the perspective of another) or strictly an emotional response (e.g., feeling another's feelings), more recently empathy has been conceptualized as involving both cognitive and emotional elements (Davis, 1983; Williams, 1990). Among therapists, Rogers (1975) saw empathy as involving being sensitive to the changing feelings of the other person while Kohut (1984) considered it an attempt to experience the inner life of another. Both Rogers and Kohut emphasized the need to maintain a distinction between self and other, implying that the therapist should take an objective stance. The latter condition seems contrary to the definitions of most of the writers who study empathy in contexts other than therapy. For these researchers, the affective responses of the observer are crucial. In this regard Eisenberg, in several of her articles (Eisenberg & Fabes, 1990; Eisenberg, Murphy, & Shepard, 1997; Eisenberg, Shea, Carlo, & Knight, 1991; Eisenberg & Strayer, 1987), identifies the affective response in empathy as a match, or nearly so, for the observed person's emotion. Marshall, Hudson, Jones, and Fernandez (1995) made the same claim in their multi-stage

conceptualization of empathy. There is, in fact, no reason to demand this and every reason to suppose that the emotional reaction to another person's state could be quite different and yet still
be empathic. Sometimes, when we see a person crying, it evokes
a tearful response in us; at other times it evokes compassion.
And yet both seem to involve empathy. As we have learned, some
authors claim that empathy can produce such distress in the observer that he or she simply wants to escape the situation. This is
because the definition of empathy employed by these authors is
primarily cognitive in nature and is limited to the recognition of
distress. Miller and Eisenberg (1988) take a strictly emotional
view, defining empathy as "an emotional response evoked by the
affective state or situation of the other person" (p. 325).

In her work with children, Ainsworth (1973) includes in her definition of empathy the ability to share and understand another
child's emotions and to recognize the signals that indicate their
feeling state. She clearly sees empathy as having both cognitive/
perceptual components and affective responses. Similarly, both
Aronfreed (1968) and Feshbach (1978) suggest that empathy involves both the ability to take another person's perspective and
the emotional responses evoked by observing the other's feelings.
As noted, both Davis (1983) and William's (1990) took a multi-
component view of empathy. Davis described four components
that together made up the empathic response: perspective taking,
fantasy, empathic concern, and personal distress. While this was
a step in the right direction and produced a multi-component
measure that has proved useful, Davis did not make clear how
these components interacted.

Marshall et al. (1995) outlined a multi-stage model of empathy
that explicitly pointed to the relationship between the stages.
Their model had four stages with each stage being dependent
upon the preceding stage: (1) recognition of another person's
emotional state; (2) taking the perspective of the other person;

(3) experiencing the same or similar emotion as the observed person; and, (4) taking some action to ameliorate the other person's distress. It has already been noted that the third stage does not have to be a replication of the observed person's state but can simply be feelings of compassion. While the observations by Batson et al. (1987) and by Hanson (1997; Hanson & Scott, 1995), indicated that emotional recognition does not always result in compassionate or helping behavior (i.e., what many call sympathy), and in such instances, we would not consider the responses to be empathic. For Marshal et al. sympathy is described by the two latter stages of their model, that is, feelings of distress or compassion that motivate helping behavior. The whole process, however, defines empathy. To complete the picture, it is necessary to consider all the responses that might be made as a result of observing the distress of another person. Appendix One illustrates these possible responses and represents an adaptation of Batson et al.'s (1987) model to accommodate Hanson's (1997) observations and Marshall et al.'s (1995) views on empathy. It is only the lower sequence that we would call empathy.

Empathy, from our perspective, involves first, the ability to accurately perceive the emotional state of another person (emotional recognition); second, the ability to see things as the other person sees them (perspective taking); third, the capacity to respond emotionally to the other person's distress (empathic responding); and, finally, the enactment of some compassionate response (sympathy). The latter may take the form of attempting to ameliorate the other person's distress, or, when responding to a character in a book, play, or movie, the experience of feeling a desire to help.

Marshall et al.'s model, ultimately shown to be correct, has the advantage of directing research to examine the capacity of clients to respond appropriately at each stage. For example, we (Hudson et al; 1993) have found deficits in the ability of sexual offenders to accurately identify the emotional states of others, and Hanson and Scott (1995) have found these offenders are poor at perspec-tive-taking. Quite clearly, sexual offenders do not display sympa-thy toward their victims during their offending behaviors, and their most marked deficits in empathy are toward their own vic-tims (Fernandez & Marshall, in press; Fernandez et al., 1999).

Pithers (1999) has offered salient criticisms of our model that need to be mentioned. Remember that our model is a stage model; whereby, each stage requires successful completion of the prior stage. As Pithers notes, some compassionate (altruistic) acts are rapid immediate responses (e.g., dragging an uncon-scious person from a burning vehicle) that could not be preceded by the processes we proposed in our model (e.g., in the example it would not be possible to recognize the emotional responses of an unconscious person). Perhaps we should have described the first stage as simply involving the recognition of distress. Sec-ondly, Pithers points out that empathic people try to anticipate the other person's emotional response to what the empathic per-son might say or do so as to avoid upsetting them. Empathic people do this rather than acting then waiting for a response that might be distressful. There are, in fact, two extensive bodies of research relevant to this notion of anticipating another's re-sponse: anticipatory active planning (Goody, 1995) and empathic accuracy (Ickes, 1997). Anticipatory active planning is one aspect of social intelligence and is covered in detail in Chapter 5 of this book. Empathic accuracy requires the observer not only to accu-rately infer another's behavior but also to predict the other person's responses to the observer's behavior.

Some adjustments to our model, then, appear to be required. How readily a model can adapt to feedback from research deter-mines, at least up to a point, its merit. Future research, we ex-pect, will continue to provide refinements to various models of empathy, and as a result, our attempts to measure it will improve as will our efforts to enhance empathic responding.

The Measurement of Empathy

G. Serran

"The work of science is to substitute facts for apprearances, and demonstrations for impressions." John Ruskin (1819-1900)

Empathy has been considered a foundation of many of the helping professions, including clinical psychology, nursing, occupational therapy, social work, and counseling to name a few. Given the importance of the concept of empathy in a variety of areas, effective measurement and conceptualization is critical. The chosen measurement of empathy differs across studies based on the researcher's conceptualization of empathy and on the direction of his or her research. As a consequence, researchers have used various self-report measures as well as physical indices of empathy. However, reviews of the literature indicate that little consensus exists on exactly what constitutes empathy, and very little has been done to consolidate the theories and definitions.

The use of various procedures to measure empathy make it difficult to compare different studies so that inferences cannot be drawn about the nature of empathy and its effects. In fact, perhaps the most pressing issue in the study of empathy that needs to be addressed concerns an agreed upon definition and measure. In Chapter 1 of this book offered a conceptualization of the nature of empathy that allows for the measurement of its various stages or components, but as yet, we have not made sufficient progress in developing a measure.

As noted in Chapter 1, empathy has traditionally been seen as either a cognitive process (i.e., the ability to take another's perspective) or as an emotional process (i.e., the ability to experience the feelings of another). The Hogan Empathy Scale (Hogan, 1969) typifies cognitive approaches to measuring empathy while the Questionnaire Measure of Emotional Empathy (Mehrabian & Epstein, 1972), is a popular measure of emotional empathy. In addition to the "cognitive versus emotional" debate about empathy, it has been construed as a "trait" (i.e., consistently evident across time, people, and places) by some researchers/theorists and as a "state" (i.e., dependent upon current circumstances) by others [see Cottrell (1942) for a discussion of this issue specific to empathy, and Mischel (1968) for a more general discussion of traits versus states]. Most current measures of empathy treat it as a trait, and indeed, there is some evidence of cross-person consistency (Marangomi, Garcia, Ickes, & Teng, 1995). However, there is also evidence that various features (situational and personal) modify empathic responding (Batson, 1987). It seems likely that the best measures of empathy will allow for the influence of these various unstable factors.

The following section will review a number of the available empathy measures followed by a section focusing on specific measures used to determine therapist empathy and then by a section on the measurement of empathy in sexual offender populations.

GENERAL MEASURES OF EMPATHY

As mentioned previously, the general measures of empathy typically construe empathy as a trait manifested toward all people across all situations. As noted, this view is not entirely consistent with the evidence and does not appear to match our everyday experiences (see Chapter 1 for examples). The problems inherent in defining empathy should be kept in mind when considering the available measures. Given the inconsistent definitions of empathy found in the literature, it is unlikely that any of the measures discussed below assess empathy in a manner that would satisfy everyone. In fact, Deutsch and Madle (1975) advised that "in the event that new measures are developed, attempts should be made to incorporate the various concepts of empathy. It is only through the recognition that empathy measures may not represent a single construct, but rather multiple and perhaps related constructs that more valid measures can be developed than in the past" (p.277). We believe the way we construed empathy in Chapter 1 might serve as a basis for generating measures that meet Deutsch and Madle's criterion. If we are to improve our ability to measure empathy, it is important to understand what each currently available scale purports to measure and to have a good understanding of the strengths and weaknesses of the available measures. For a more detailed summary of this issue, see Chlopan, McCain, Carbonell, and Hagen (1985).

George Washington Social Intelligence Test

As mentioned earlier in this chapter, this measure has been widely used in the social intelligence literature. Social intelligence has been defined as the ability to get along with others, to have knowledge of social issues, and to have insight into the temporary moods or personality traits of others (Vernon, 1933). This definition appears to overlap with most definitions of empathy; thus, social intelligence measures have been used in some reports to measure empathy. The items included in the George Washington Social Intelligence Test fall into five categories:

1) judgments made in social situations, 2) memory for names and faces, 3) accuracy in observing human behavior, 4) recognition of the mental state of another, 5) a sense of humor.

Research has provided some support for the validity of this test (Hunt, 1927; Vernon, 1933); however, McClatchy (1929) criticized this research for failing to show that the George Washington Scale measured anything other than verbal intelligence.

Chapin Social Insight Test

Chapin (1942) developed a 45-item test to measure social insight. Each item on the test presents a social situation and requires a choice from four alternatives of either the most insightful commentary or the wisest course of action, depending on the situation. When initial tests of validity were not satisfactory, 20 items were removed and the test was revised.

Gough (1965) conducted a number of validity studies on this scale using groups of males and females from different occupations and with different educational status. Based on Gough's research, the test appears to be effective in separating groups in terms of social insight (e.g., effective and noneffective leaders, good versus poor listeners, accurate from inaccurate observers, and perceptive versus nonperceptive individuals). High scorers were described as active, alert, and capable, while low scorers were pessimistic, unable to commit themselves to a course of action, and uncertain in their relationships. It is unclear as to why this test has not received a great deal of attention from empathy researchers; however, this lack of attention limits conclusions regarding its usefulness.

Dymond Rating Test of Insight and Empathy

Using the definition of empathy as the imaginative transposing of oneself into the thinking, feeling, and acting of another, Dymond (1949; 1950) developed Rating Test A and Rating Test B. Both tests require the individual to rate both himself and another subject from both his perspective and from the perspective of the other person. A 5-point scale is used for each of six traits. The six traits are: 1) superior-inferior; 2) friendly-unfriendly; 3) leader-follower; 4) self-confidence; 5) selfish-unselfish; 6) sense of humor. In test B, the last 3 traits have been replaced by: shy-self assured, sympathetic-nonsympathetic, and secure-insecure. Early research by Dymond offered rather weak support for the validity of the test and indicated that high scorers were better adjusted on personality tests. However, Lindgren and Robinson (1953) suggested that instead of empathizing, subjects might be responding to the cultural imperative that people should consistently maintain certain attitudes. In addition, the administration is difficult and lengthy, requiring over two hours. These factors contribute to the lack of popularity of this scale in measuring empathy.

Empathy Test

Kerr and Speroff (1954) constructed their measure based on the assumption that empathic individuals are superior in their ability to anticipate the reactions, feelings, and behaviors of others. The test requires subjects to rank: the popularity of 15 types of music for a defined type of worker; the national circulation of 15 magazines; and the prevalence of 10 types of annoyances for a defined individual.

Hall (1965) and Thorndike (1959), in their surveys of the literature, concluded that the evidence supporting the validity of this test is inconclusive. Since empathy is generally defined as an interpersonal process, the ranking of preferences and annoyances of an unknown individual has little face validity, and overall, there is little evidence to justify the claim that this is a measure of empathy.

Hogan Empathy Scale

Prior to developing his scale, Hogan provided 14 laypersons with the dictionary definition of empathy and asked them to describe a highly empathic man. He found a high degree of consistency across these 14 subjects, from which Hogan concluded that empathy is a recognizable and meaningful construct.

Hogan validated the criteria provided by his 14 subjects and began selecting items for his measure, providing a 64-item scale. He (Hogan, 1969) reported extensive analyses of reliability and validity conducted among eleven groups of men and three groups of women (N=1086). Extensive subsequent research has been conducted with this measure relating empathy to personality characteristics, moral conduct, and to the prediction of behavior in various situations.

Several studies have examined the relationship between scores on the Hogan Empathy Scale and scores on measures of anxiety, autonomy, and locus of control. For example, prisoners who scored higher on empathy were less anxious (Andrews, Wormith, Daigle-Zinn, Kennedy, & Nelson, 1981). Similarly, Kupfer, Drew, Curtis, and Rubinstein (1978) found significant negative correlations between high scores on the empathy measure and anxiety. Further studies examining the relationship between responses to this test and various personality variables have shown that high scorers have humanistic reasons for choosing caregiving careers and are rated as more likeable, more extroverted, and more disclosing (Hogan, 1969; Hogan & Mankin, 1970; Streit-Forest, 1982).

One consistent finding is that those supposedly lacking in morality score lower on the Hogan's scale. For example, Gendreau, Burke, and Grant (1980) found that inmates who chose to work with disadvantaged people had higher scores than those who chose not to volunteer to help. Delinquents tend to score lower than nondelinquents (Kurtines & Hogan, 1972) and repeat offenders score lower than nonprisoners and first-time offenders. Lack of empathy also appears to predict abusive mothering (Letourneau, 1981).

In summary, Hogan's Empathy Scale was designed to measure the ability of an individual to see things from another person's point of view. According to Hogan, empathic people are more socially aware, better adjusted, and care more about the feelings of others. A factor analysis of the Hogan Scale (Johnson, Check, & Struther, 1983) revealed four factors: social self-confidence, even-temperedness, sensitivity, and nonconformity. The negative relationship (noted above) between scores on Hogan's Empathy Scale and criminal behavior might be a function of the sensitivity and even-temperedness components, while sensitivity, social awareness, and even-temperedness may explain why empathic people have been rated as better adjusted and more socially aware.

In contrast, more recent research has brought into question the usefulness of this measure. Cross and Sharpley (1982) pointed out that little research has been published on the reliability of the Hogan Empathy Scale. In Cross and Sharpley's study the test was administered to 95 subjects and resulted in an alpha coefficient of .61, which was not considered satisfactory. Additionally, 13 items were found to correlate negatively with the total score, suggesting these items were not measuring empathy as defined by the scale. Furthermore, 30 items did not correlate with the total score at a reasonable level. Froman and Peloquin (2000) attempted to determine the reliability, internal consistency, factor structure, and convergent and discriminant validity of Hogan's scale with occupational therapy students. A total of 320 participants completed the measure on one occasion, and smaller subgroups (n=192) and (n=56) completed it again on either two or three later occasions in time. Test-retest reliability was found to be modest, while internal consistency was reported as alpha = .57, which is far lower than the .80 generally accepted as the recommended value for established scales (Nunnally & Bernstein, 1994). Using principal components analysis and factor analyses, Froman and Peloquin were not able to replicate the four-factor solution reported by Johnson et al. (1983). Validity was tested by Froman and Peloquin by examining the relationship between variables conceptually similar to empathy (convergent validity) and those independent of empathy (discriminate validity). Empathy was not found strongly related to those performance evaluations that should correspond with empathy. In addition, empathy was not related to age, gender, or to academic achievement.

In summary, the reliability estimates of Hogan's Empathy Scale were disappointing, and these results do not support the value of this measure. Overall the empirical evaluations of Hogan's Empathy Scale suggest that the usefulness of this scale for measuring empathy may be questionable.

The Questionnaire Measure of Emotional Empathy

Mehrabian and Epstein (1972) pointed out that most measures of empathy, available at the time of their writing, did not adequately account for the empathic emotional response. As a result, they developed a new measure. Their Questionnaire Measure of Emotional Empathy is a 33-item test requiring the respondent to rate each item on a scale from −4 (very strong disagreement) to +4 (very strong agreement). High scores indicate high empathy, although females consistently score higher than males.

The intercorrelated subscales and sample items include: susceptibility to emotional contagion ("The people around me have a
great influence on my moods"); appreciation of the feelings of
unfamiliar and distant others ("Lonely people are probably un-
friendly"); extreme emotional responsiveness ("Sometimes the
words of a love song move me deeply"); tendency to be moved by
other's positive emotional experiences ("Another's laughter is not
catching for me"); tendency to be moved by others' negative emotional experiences ("Seeing people cry upsets me"); sympathetic
tendency ("It is hard for me to see how some things upset people
so much"); and willingness to be in contact with others who have
problems ("I would rather be a social worker than work at a job
training center"). Both Mehrabian and Epstein (1972) and
Adams, Schvaneveldt, and Jenson (1979) found evidence that the
scale was internally consistent. Additionally, Mehrabian and
Epstein (1972) found that empathy modified aggressive behavior
in a mock situation, and it facilitated helping behavior.

Davis' Interpersonal Reactivity Index

Support for the notion of empathy as a multidimensional construct suggests that empathy may be a process, involving both
perspective-taking and affective processes (Coke, Batson, &
McDavis, 1978). Based on speculation that our understanding of
empathy can improve only by integrating the affective and cognitive components, Davis (1983) developed a measure of empathy
with four subscales. Davis' measure is a 28-item, self-report
measure consisting of four, 7-item subscales, each tapping some
aspect of the global concept of empathy. The Perspective-Taking
scale (PT) assesses the tendency to adopt the psychological viewpoint of others; the Fantasy scale (FS) measures the tendency to
imagine oneself in the role of fictitious characters in movies,
books, or plays; The Empathic Concern scale (EC) assesses
"other-oriented" feelings of sympathy and concern; and the Per-

sonal Distress scale (PD) measures self-oriented feelings of anxiety or tension in difficult interpersonal situations. Earlier investigations of empathy (Coke et al., 1978) suggested that these constructs are potentially important aspects of empathy, as research supports the link between emotional responses and helping behavior. The content domain of each subscale reflects the variety of reactions to others that have been referred to as "empathy" within the literature.

Davis (1983) investigated the validity of the four subscales by examining their relationship with other constructs (social competence/interpersonal functioning, self-esteem, emotionality, sensitivity to others, and intelligence) as well as their relationship to both Hogan's Empathy Scale and the Mehrabian and Epstein Empathy Scale. The cognitive Hogan scale was most highly correlated with the cognitive PT scale, and the least association with the Mehrabian and Epstein scale. The FS and EC scales displayed substantially greater associations with the Mehrabian and Epstein Empathy Scale. Research also supports the reliability and stability of the four scales.

Measurement of Empathy for Specific Populations

A great deal of attention has been paid to the relationship between empathy and both aggressive and helping behavior. The assumption appears to be that those who behave aggressively lack empathy while those high in empathy will be more likely to engage in prosocial or helping behavior. This assumption has led clinicians and researchers who work with specific client populations (such as men and women who abuse their children and men who abuse their partners) to attempt to evaluate empathy (or lack of empathy) in these particular clients. In contrast, individuals such as therapists, particularly those who choose to work with troubled clients, are often assumed to be highly empathic. As a consequence, some researchers have attempted to measure therapist empathy and determine its relation to treatment outcome. The following section will focus on the measurement of empathy in some specific populations, in this case, therapists and sexual offenders. It is important to note that the psychometric properties of most of these measures are unclear.

Measurement of Empathy in Therapists

Considerable research has supported a positive relationship between therapist empathy and effective therapy (e.g., Katz, 1962; Rogers, Gendlin, Kiesler, & Truax, 1967; Truax & Carkhuff, 1967). However, as in the general literature, these studies have used many different means of conceptualizing and measuring empathy, which severely limits any conclusions that can be made from the literature. In fact, those studies that have compared different measures of therapist empathy have found little to suggest a close relationship between these measures (Hansen, Moore, & Carkhuff, 1968; Katz, 1962; Truax, 1966). The majority of the quantitative research has involved recording sessions and having judges listen to session fragments in order to make inferences about the therapist's empathy.

SPECIFIC MEASURES OF THERAPIST EMPATHY.
Truax's (1961) Accurate Empathy Scale, Barrett-Lennard's (1962) Relationship Inventory Scales, and Carkhuff's (1969) Empathic Understanding Scale were all based on Rogers' (1957; 1959) conceptualization of therapist empathy (i.e., to perceive the client as the client sees himself). In contrast, Katz's (1962) Predictive Empathy measure is based on a cognitive, role-taking approach to empathy.

One of the most commonly used measures in psychotherapy research is the Empathic Understanding Scale developed by Carkhuff (1969), modified from Truax's (1961) Accurate Empathy Scale. These scales were developed specifically to evaluate therapist empathy and involve listening to segments of therapist sessions and rating them based on different affect levels and content areas. Responses are rated by trained judges, and research suggests high interrater reliabilities (Engram & Vandergoot, 1978). However, Bachrach (1976) suggests that often what is being judged may not be "empathy" as conceptualized by the clinical literature but rather other characteristics such as warmth of the therapist, skill, or a global "good" quality (Rappaport & Chinsky, 1972). Additionally, other researchers have questioned the construct validity of these scales, pointing out that only the therapist's rather than the client's response is considered.

These measures may also be classified according to whether they are subjective, objective, or predictive. Subjective measures are those based on the therapist's or client's perception of the session (e.g., the Truax Relationship Inventory), objective measures use external independent judgements (e.g., Truax's Accurate Empathy Scale), while predictive measures assume that empathy exists if predictions can be made about how others might respond to certain conditions or stimuli. For example, Katz's (1962) Predictive Empathy measures the therapist's predictions of his client on the Self-Concept Q-Sort. Thus, conclusions regarding therapist empathy are largely dependent on the approach used to measure empathy.

In an attempt to deal with these problems, Kurtz and Grummon (1972) compared six different methods of measuring empathy with a therapy process variable and several outcome measures. They measured empathy using several different approaches:

1) Situational Measure

   Kurtz and Grummon used a standardized test (The Affective Sensitivity Scale; Kagan et al., 1967) to measure the ability of the therapist to perceive and identify affective states in others (an important component of empathy). In this approach, empathy is viewed as a trait such that therapists who score high on the measure are perceived as being more empathic. This measure uses videotaped segments of actual sessions, and therapists are required to respond to 89 multiple-choice items based on the feelings expressed by the client.

2) Predictive Measures

   This approach had the therapist predict how the client would respond on a personality inventory. Two predictive measures were obtained, utilizing several client self-descriptive measures.

3) Judged Tape Ratings

   In this approach, independent judges rated the level of therapist empathy. Carkhuff's Empathic Understanding in Interpersonal Process Scale (1969) was used by the judges, who rated segments of both early and later sessions.

4) Perceived Empathy

   The client's perception of therapist empathy was obtained using the Barrett-Lennard (1962) Relationship Inventory, which was completed after the third and the final therapy sessions. Items on the scale included "He tries to see things through my eyes" and "He understands my words but not the way I feel." On the therapist form of this scale, therapists rated their own level of empathy.

5) The Process Measure

   Each therapy case was rated by two judges, using Carkhuff and Berenson's (1967) Self-Exploration in Inter personal Process Scale. This scale categorizes the session according to different levels, based on the client's willingness to disclose feelings and experiences.

6) Outcome Measures

   Outcome measures were collected approximately one week after the completion of therapy. These included a self-report scale of client change, judges' ratings on pre- and post-treatment MMPI scores, and therapist and client judgements of client progress.

The measures of therapist empathy described above are representative of the approaches used in previous psychotherapy and counseling research, and all of these measures purport to assess the same or a similar variable, namely therapist empathy. Unfortunately, the correlations among the measures reported in this study were low and insignificant, with several measures being negatively correlated. Therapist empathy may be more difficult to measure than it appears. In terms of outcome, no relationship was found between predictive empathy and outcome. Additionally, clients and independent judges disagreed with the therapist. This certainly calls into question the ability of therapists to accurately rate their own empathy skills.

Truax and Carkhuff (1967) reviewed a number of studies that supported the relationship between tape-judged empathy and outcome, and Krutz and Grummon (1972) found similar results (e.g., judgements of empathy from videotaped segments was related to self-exploration). Client-perceived empathy, on the other hand, was shown by Krutz and Grummon to have the strongest relationship with outcome than any of the empathy measures. Based on their results, Kurtz and Grummon (1972) questioned the idea that therapist empathy can be successfully measured. However, it is clear that empathy is related to outcome, and it appears that judges' ratings and the client's perceptions may be important determinates. Unfortunately, present measures may be tapping other aspects of the therapist's behavior (e.g., warmth), suggesting that clear definitions and even clearer measures of therapist empathy are required.

Generalized Empathy in Sexual Offenders

Hanson (in press) described four methods that have been used to assess empathy in sexual offenders: 1) inferences made from their offense and social history, 2) direct observations, 3) measures of cognitive distortions, and 4) self-report empathy measures. The most common general measures of empathy used with sexual offenders have been the Hogan Empathy Scale, the Emotional Empathy Scale, and Davis' Interpersonal Reactivity Index. Unfortunately, the evidence for generalized empathy deficits among sexual offenders is less than compelling. Using the Hogan Empathy Scale, a group of rapists incarcerated in a maximum security hospital were found to be less empathic than a group of nonoffending males (Rice, Chaplin, Harris, & Coutts, 1990, 1994). However, these results were not replicated in a later study by Seto (1992) who found that when level of education was covaried out, the differences disappeared.

Langevin, Wright, and Handy (1988) found that scores on the Mehrabian and Epstein Emotional Empathy Scale did not discriminate between 96 mixed sexual offenders and a normative sample of college students. Sexual offender subgroups were not differentiated by total empathy scores or by any of the items, and empathy scores were not related to violence. Similarly, Hoppe and Singer (1976) found that this scale did not distinguish sexual offenders from other types of offenders. Rice, Chaplin, Harris, and Coutts (1994) found no differences between rapists and community subjects on this measure.

Pithers (1994), using the Davis Interpersonal Reactivity Index, found that rapists demonstrated less empathy than pedophiles and that the scores for both groups increased following victim empathy training. However, the average scores for both groups at pre-treatment were the same as those found with normative subjects. Hayashino, Wurtele, and Klebe (1995) found no differences in empathy between incest offenders, extrafamilial child molesters, incarcerated nonsexual offenders, and community subjects on any of the various scales they employed. Hanson (in press) suggested that while the Perspective-Taking and Empathic Concern subscales of Davis' measure have promise in the assessment of empathy in sexual offenders, they might be too general. In fact, based on the available research, it appears that sexual offenders do not suffer from generalized empathy deficits. Researchers have, therefore, begun to focus on identifying particular persons or situations where sexual offenders are more or less likely to display empathy.

In this respect, McGrath, Cann, and Konopasky (1998) developed the Empat, which assesses both general and victim-specific empathy. The Empat consists of 45 items to which the offender responds on a 5-point Likert scale from strongly agree to strongly disagree. Initial research on this measure suggested that sexual offenders, even after being instructed to fake good, displayed less empathy for sexual abuse victims compared to male college students, although general empathy was similar between groups. Hennessy, Walter, and Vess (2002) compared patients who were civilly committed under California's Sexually Violent Predator law to the groups in McGrath et al's (1998) sample. They found that the rapists and child molesters in their sample scored significantly higher in victim empathy than any of the original sex offender groups, and rapists scored higher than the male college students. The clinicians administering the measure concluded that the measure was too easily manipulated by patients. Again, these findings suggest the need for more adequate measures.

Measurement of Victim Empathy in Sexual Offenders

Marshall, Hudson, Jones, and Fernandez (1995) recommended that researchers focus on victim-specific empathy, suggesting that the majority of sexual offenders should display empathy in a variety of non-offense related circumstances. Several measures have been developed to assist in determining what specific empathy deficits may exist. Hanson and Scott (1995) designed the Empathy for Women and Empathy for Children tests in which written vignettes are used to assess perspective-taking deficits in sexual offenders. The tests contain 15 vignettes describing interactions between men and women or between adults and children. Fernandez and her colleagues (Fernandez & Marshall, in press; Fernandez, Marshall, Lightbody, & O'Sullivan, 1999) developed separate empathy measures for child molesters and rapists. These measures require subjects to identify harmful effects to a victim who has experienced sexual abuse or some other non-sexual trauma. Other measures include having rapists rate the reactions of women in videotaped vignettes of dating situations (Lipton, McDonel, & McFall, 1987; Murphy, Coleman, & Haynes, 1986) and having child molesters respond to written descriptions of adult and child sexual interactions (Beckett, Beech, Fisher, & Fordham, 1994; Stermac & Segal, 1989).

In an evaluation of emotional recognition skills, Hudson et al. (1993) found that sexual offenders and violent offenders had difficulty accurately identifying surprise, fear, anger, and disgust in others. Scully (1988) found that although 58% of the rapists in her study acknowledged some understanding of the victims' feelings and were able to respond emotionally to this recognition, they had no empathy for the victims. Level of empathy also appears to be related to attitudes and behavior regarding sexual assault; those who display high empathy toward rape victims express a lower likelihood of actually committing rape (Deitz, Blackwell, Daley, & Bentley, 1982) while low empathy males are more likely to blame the victim for the assault and to see the offense as less serious than males displaying high victim empathy (Deitz, Littman, & Bentley, 1984).

Using written vignettes of adult and child sexual interactions, Stermac and Segal (1989) found that child molesters, relative to rapists and nonoffenders, tended to underestimate the child's distress. Beckett et al. (1994) found that child molesters underestimated the harmfulness of sexual offenses, suggesting that child molesters lack empathy for the victim. In an attempt to control for any self-report biases with their measures, Hanson and Scott (1995) included a variety of descriptions of interactions, some of which were abusive, some not, and others ambiguous. On their Empathy for Women test, rapists tended to underestimate the woman's distress in the vignettes compared to other groups, while on the Child Molester version, treated child molesters were more accurate than an untreated group at identifying victim distress.

Fernandez et al. (1999) designed a Child Molester Empathy Measure that examines empathy toward three different children: 1) a child who has been disfigured in an accident, 2) a child who has been sexually abused by an unspecified assailant, and 3) the offenders' own victim(s). Research utilizing this measure suggests it is internally consistent and has good test-retest reliability. Compared to nonoffenders, child molesters displayed less empathy toward the child who had been sexually abused by another offender. However, the greatest empathy deficits were apparent in the child molesters attitudes toward their own victim(s) (Fernandez et al., 1999; Marshall, Champagne, Brown, & Miller, 1997; Marshall, Champagne, Sturgeon & Bryce, 1997; Marshall, Hamilton, & Fernandez, 1998; Marshall, O'Sullivan, & Fernandez, 1996).

Fernandez and Marshall (in press) modified this measure for rapists, evaluating empathy toward women across the same circumstances as the child measure. Interestingly, rapists demonstrated more empathy toward the accident victim compared to a group of nonsexual offenders, and they showed the same degree of empathy toward the victim of sexual assault. Similar to the findings with child molesters, rapists displayed lower empathy toward their own victim(s).

Overall, empathy deficits apparent among sexual offenders are likely to be specific to their own victims, as opposed to them having generalized empathy problems. Recent research, however, suggests that these "deficits" may not reflect problems with empathy at all but rather are manifestations of cognitive distortions that are specific to the victim and are used to justify their offensive behavior (Hanson, in press; Hilton, 1993). In fact, the existing victim-specific questionnaires include items that could be interpreted as cognitive distortions (e.g., victims are not harmed by the experience). Again, further research is necessary to tease out the types and degree of deficits in empathy that do exist. In sexual offenders, for example, sadistic offenders or psychopaths may be expected to fall into the category of "hostile toward the distressed person" in the model of empathy outlined in Chapter 1 of this book. In that case these particular offenders may derive pleasure from the suffering of their victims rather than feel empathy toward them. Continued focus is encouraged on the development of appropriate measures and further research is clearly required.

Conclusions

Based on the above review, it does not appear that any strong conclusions regarding the appropriateness of the available empathy measures can be made. The main obstacle to designing and choosing a measure appears to be the lack of consistency regarding the conceptualization of empathy. In fact, prior to developing and refining existing measures, ensuring that everyone is measuring the same thing is critical. On the brighter side, many of the features that make up empathy have been agreed upon, suggesting that developing a standardized approach is not beyond our reach.

A multidimensional approach to empathy appears to be the most logical way to proceed; it is unlikely that a single mechanism (e.g., only cognitive or only emotional) accounts for what we conceive of as "empathy." Nevertheless, many unanswered questions remain, and only further research will help determine which scales best measure empathy. The obvious first step should be to develop a standard definition of empathy, so that researchers are more consistent in their understanding of what they are attempting to measure. The conceptualization of the empathic process outlined in the figure in Chapter 1 of this book represents our attempt to offer a definition that, combined with the staged model we designed earlier (Marshall et al., 1995), provides a model for developing appropriate measures. These measures, we suggest, should be specific to both persons (e.g., victims), and to the stages of empathy (e.g., recognition of distress in others, perspective-taking). In this regard, we reject the question of assessing empathy as a trait that is apparent across situations, time, and persons.

3

The Development of Empathy

L. Marshall

"The beginning is the most important part of any work,
expecially in the case of a young and tender thing;
for that is the time at which the character is being formed and
the desired impression is more readily taken." Plato (427?-347)

In their movie *The Meaning of Life*, Monty Python concluded the meaning of life to be "try to be nice to people; avoid eating fat; read a good book every now and then; get some walking in; and try to live together in peace and harmony with people of all creeds and nations" (Goldstone & Jones, 1983). Although the Pythons intended to use this definition of the meaning of life as comedy, two of their components (i.e., try to be nice to people and try to live together in peace and harmony with people of all creeds and nations) underline the fact that, as humans, we live in social groups and are concerned with the well-being of other members of our species. An important question for psychologists, then, is how and why does this capacity to be sensitive to other humans (and animals) develop?

As will be demonstrated later in this chapter, in order to function effectively and to maximize the benefits of living within a social group, animals, including humans, must minimize the amount of conflict and enhance bonds with other group members (Brothers, 1990). An awareness of the affect of other group members can contribute to this goal. One way to achieve this is to be able to accurately perceive and show regard for the feelings of others, namely display empathy.

The current examination of the development of empathy is not meant to be exhaustive. Much research has been done and much has been written on the development of empathy and its related constructs (Eisenberg & Strayer, 1987; Moore, 1990). Unfortunately, despite the large body of research that focuses on empathy, the developmental literature on empathy suffers from a variety of limitations, not the least of which is that much of this research is based on varying definitions of empathy. As a consequence, the development of empathy in humans has yet to be satisfactorily explained (Thomson, 1987). For the purposes of the current examination of the development of empathy, however, W. L. Marshall's adapted view of empathy presented elsewhere in this book will be used.

MODEL OF EMPATHY

According to W. L. Marshall's view, empathy involves: 1) recognizing the emotional state of others experiencing distress, 2) recognizing the issue from the other person's perspective, 3) being able to experience a compassionate feeling or a feeling similar to the other person, and 4) taking action to reduce the other person's distress. Marshall's definition of the construct of empathy is comprehensive and suggests testable hypotheses.

Marshall's definition of empathy clearly has implications for the developmental age of "full-blown" empathy. His definition requires the empathizer to have sophisticated perceptual abilities and mature affective, cognitive, and locomotor abilities. That is, the actor must not only recognize that others have emotions (i.e., distress), he or she must also feel some distress for the other person, must understand what that distress feels like, and, perhaps critically, be able to or desire to act in order to reduce the other person's distress. This, as we will see, has implications for the age at which we can say empathy develops.

In order to simplify this examination of the development of empathy, I will present research and theory from a number of different perspectives in an order that I hope makes developmental sense. What is interesting from a developmental perspective are questions such as "Is empathy learned or is it an innate ability? At what age does empathy appear?" And, "How is empathy affected by environmental factors?" Therefore, we will start our examination with a review of the developmental literature on an innate basis for empathy. Then, we will turn to the earliest precursor of empathy, that is, the perception of others. Once we have established that the distress of others can be detected, then we can look at how the affective and cognitive aspects of empathy develop. Finally we will look at the correlates of a failure to successfully develop empathy.

Evolution and Empathy

A belief that there is an inherent capacity or mechanism for empathy has been suggested since the nineteenth century and has reappeared in more recent research (e.g., Brothers, 1990; Hoffman, 1981; Plutchik, 1980; 1983). In order to find support for an evolutionary view of empathy, it is necessary to examine whether animals exhibit behavior that is analogous to empathy in humans and to explain the enhanced survival function of empathic behavior (Plutchik, 1987). Given the complexity of Marshall's adapted model of empathy and sympathy, it seems unlikely that non-human animals can display the full range of cognitive and affective abilities necessary to be empathic or sympathetic. However, Plutchik (1983), Brothers (1990), and Hoffman

(1990) report that non-human animals do engage in behaviors that are the precursors of empathic behavior. For example, the perceptual ability needed to detect affect in others is a precursor to empathic behavior.

In an effort to support the hypothesis of an evolutionary basis for empathy, Brothers (1990) cites research on brain organization in primates, which demonstrates a neural circuitry for rapid processing of facial and gestural information. Brothers points out that relations with others are important for primates' reproduction and survival, and, therefore, the ability to read the affect of other social group members is advantageous. She also reports research which demonstrates the ability of chimpanzees to attribute seeing, wanting, and expecting to others, which are, according to Premack (1988), early elements of a "Theory of Mind." The human ability to generate theories about other's mental activities (e.g., intentions, desires, beliefs, emotions, etc.) has been referred to as "Theory of Mind" (Lee, 2000). Children's acquisition of a theory of mind has been researched under two main areas: 1) appearance-reality distinction, in which an object's or person's appearance may be different from reality (e.g., food may look good but is actually poisonous, or a person may look nice but is actually a criminal) and 2) false-belief understanding, in which people may have a false belief about the world and behave erroneously based on that belief (e.g., that it is warm outside in winter because they see the sun shining and, therefore, fail to dress appropriately before leaving the house). Children seem to develop a theory of mind somewhere between the ages of three and five years (Gopnik & Astington, 2000).

What chimpanzees cannot do, which is why they cannot respond with empathy under Marshall's model or demonstrate Theory of Mind, is hold another's state of mind while simultaneously holding a different mental state themselves. Based on this line of evidence, Brothers (1990) argues that within the human brain, there is a module of cognition for the construction of psychological features of others. She hypothesizes that this module 1) operates on a specific domain (social) in the environment, 2) appears to follow a stereotypic ontogenetic course that is evolutionarily plausible, 3) can be isolated by neurologic impairment or innate brain dysfunction (e.g., autism and autism-like disorders such as Asperger's syndrome, capgras syndrome), and 4) is based on specifiable core operations. Brothers reports that a property of this hypothesized module is that the sensory presence of a human feature (e.g., face or voice) necessarily generates a mental perception of a person, that is, an entity with a mental life.

Plutchik (1987) reports research from a number of different sources, showing that animals display behaviors (understanding, likemindedness, sympathy, concordance and reciprocation) that are defined as synonyms for empathy by Roget's Thesaurus. He also cites examples of animal behavior patterns as evidence for the presence of empathy in other species. Plutchik (1987) suggests that animal behavior such as the schooling behavior of fish, flocking and mobbing behavior of birds, and herding behavior of mammals are indicative of mimicry and affective communication. These examples of empathy in non-human animals may not be overwhelmingly convincing to everyone that non-human animals do experience empathy. However, these examples do appear to lend credence to the idea that the capacity for empathic behavior maybe innate based on the presence of precursors to empathic behavior in non-human animals.

If we accept that the capacity for empathy-like behavior is found in non-human animals, then empathy should contribute to evolutionary success. If empathy, as an innate ability, has not been "screened out" over the many millions of years of development, it would seem that it must have some evolutionarily advantageous features.

Empathy and Evolutionary Continuance

Reproductive fitness is usually considered the basis for evolutionary continuance rather than the survival of the individual
(Simpson, 1999). Hamilton (1964) introduced the idea of inclusive fitness to explain why kin selection was a more satisfactory explanation of the evolutionary theory than the prevailing view at the
time: survival of the fittest. Hamilton (1964) saw the gene, rather
than the individual organism, as the target of natural selection.
The challenge that a reproductive fitness perspective of evolutionary processes poses to the survival-of-the-fittest perspective can best
be illustrated by the way some animals put themselves at survival
risk for the good of their social group. For example, individuals
calling out a distress signal in order to alert other members of their
social group to the threat of a predator put themselves at increased
risk for death. However, this altruistic behavior increases the
chance of survival of the other social group members of whom
some, if not most, are genetically related to the altruistic caller.
Therefore, under the natural selection perspective, it is evolutionarily advantageous to have an "altruistic gene," which is passed
down and helps to ensure the survival of the family group rather
than the survival of any individual member of the group. It would
seem, then, to be the continuance of genetic similarity that is more
evolutionarily advantageous than the survival of the individual.

Group behavior has been shown to contribute to inclusive fitness
by providing increased defense against predators (Plutchik, 1983).
Brothers (1990), Hoffman (1990), and Plutchik (1987) point to
the evolutionary advantages of mechanisms in social animals,
which allow them to accurately perceive the affect of other animals within their social group. For example, if one animal is distressed due to the presence of a predator and alerts the social
group to the danger but the other members of the group misread
this alarm as an invitation to play, then the other group members
will be put at increased rather than decreased risk. As a result,

the survival of the group is placed in jeopardy. If these social groups are to enhance inclusive fitness, then meaningful and accurate communication is essential.

THE DEVELOPMENT OF EMPATHIC PERCEPTUAL ABILITIES

In order to begin to make sense of the world, infants must perceive it (Muir & Slater, 2000). Research on the perceptual abilities of infants suggests that some senses, such as audition, develop sufficiently to be considered operational within the womb (Gagnon, Hunse, & Patrick 1988; Kisilevsky & Muir, 1991). Vision in humans becomes active at birth, develops rapidly, and seems to display a preference for faces (Karmiloff-Smith, 1996). This preference is believed to be brought about by an innate visual cortex preference for three blobs in a triangle representing the eyes and mouth (Slater, 2000). This preference for faces has survival utility for the infant by making the infant favor attending to the primary caregiver, usually the mother rather than other stimuli within the environment, and this is the basis for the infant's first social connection. As a consequence, we can say that the perceptual ability for detecting distress in others may be present very early in life. This suggests that, from a developmental perspective, the first stage in Marshall's model of empathy (recognition of others' emotions) is also the first stage to develop sufficiently to be enacted. It seems that infants are able to recognize distress in others very early, and it may have some innate basis. For example, research has shown that neonates reactively cry more often in response to other neonate's crying than they do to older children's cries, a computer simulated cry, or white noise (Martin & Clark, 1982; Sagi & Hoffman, 1976). However, this early form of awareness of distress in others does not necessarily mean that very young infants understand that others are in distress.

Detecting Emotions in Others

Infants can detect emotional information in the speech of adults at four months of age (Papousek, Bornstein, Nuzzo, Papousek, & Symmes, 2000) and display more social responses when an adult makes eye-contact (Symons, Hains, & Muir, 2000). A common procedure used to determine an infant's earliest social attention is the still-face procedure. Infants are seated in front of their mother under two conditions: the mother smiling and interacting with the infant normally (usually involves baby-talk, smiling, and eye contact) and the mother making eye contact with the infant but without smiling or moving any facial muscles (the still-face). Infants as young as five months find attending to this still-face very uncomfortable and turn their attention away from or become upset by the still-face (Symans et al., 2000). This suggests that five-month old infants have at least some capacity to differentiate their parent's facial expressions. While parent's facial expressions (such as joy, fear, interest, and anger) have been shown to be recognized by infants as young as 6 months (Walden & Ogan, 1988), 10 to 13 month old infants show the most accurate responses to parent's facial affect. It seems that younger children are most attentive to positive affective messages from their parents, and older children are most attentive to fearful messages (Walden & Ogan, 1988). In research on the accuracy of children's empathic judgments of the affect of others, three to five-year-olds appear to be most accurate when the target is depicted as similar to the child; however, the familiarity of the rest of the situation does not seem to affect the empathic accuracy of the child (Gibbs & Woll, 1985; Greenspan, Barenboim, & Chandler, 1976).

We can see, then, that children have the capacity to determine the affective state of others as young as six months of age. Overall, it would seem that infants as young as four months can detect distress in others, and by the age of one year, they are able to accurately determine the affect of others. However, children seem to be most empathically accurate when they perceive some similarity between the distressed person and themselves.

Affective Responding to the Distress of Others

It is clear from the above that very young children can accurately recognize distress in others and respond by becoming distressed themselves. Marshall's model describes empathy as culminating in an other-oriented response; therefore, an important developmental landmark is the shift from a self-focused behavioral response to an other-oriented response. How, then, do we determine when distress is a voluntary response that is demonstrative of empathy toward others?

As we have seen, the distress of others, which evokes a self-focused response is reported to appear in neonates (Hoffman, 1987). Ungerer and her colleagues (1990) report evidence showing that infants do not display other-oriented responses at 4 months but do at 12 months of age. Her research suggests that self-regulatory competence may account for the shift in response to the distress of others from self-focused to other-oriented behavior. Ungerer et al. (1990) suggest that very young children respond to the distress of others with coping strategies that are self-focused (e.g., thumb sucking) in order to regulate arousal and minimize stress. This occurs for two reasons: 1) they cannot yet differentiate themselves from others and, consequently, respond to the distress as if it where their own, and 2) they have not yet learned how to minimize their arousal to distress in the environment such that they can maintain focus on the environment while dealing with the distress. Ungerer et al. (1990) suggest this maturation happens in the following sequence: 1) very young infants respond to distress in the environment with self-focused behavior in order to withdraw from stress; 2) as infants' self-regulatory abilities mature, they can avert their attention from the distressing stimuli while still maintaining attention to the environment; and 3) the infant is able to maintain attention on the distressing stimuli without becoming over stimulated and can, therefore, maintain attention on the distress. It is in this third stage that an infant has the capability to achieve empathy under Marshall's model.

Perspective Taking

An important feature of Marshall's view of empathy is the ability to place oneself in the "shoes" of others. As infants move from an egocentric focus to a more social oriented focus, their increased social sophistication allows them to take the perspective of another. Moore (1990) describes perspective-taking as a multidimensional social-cognitive skill. He suggests three types of perspective-taking abilities that are representative of increasing social-cognitive skill: 1) perceptual, in which the infant can take the literal visual perspective of the other person, 2) social-cognitive, in which the infant is able to identify the thoughts, intentions, motives or social behavior of others, and 3) affective, in which the infant is able to infer other's feelings, reactions, or concerns.

Hoffman (1987) describes developmental differences in response to the distress of others from a cognitive perspective and, similar to Marshall's model, places restrictions on when we can say empathic responding occurs. For example, Hoffman also describes empathy as involving an empathic response but notes that empathic affect is experienced differently as the child develops through four main stages of a cognitive sense of others. The first stage of this model sees the child as being unable to differentiate between self and others and, consequently, the child will only respond to the distress of others, with personal distress. It appears that children experience this response to the distress of others for most of the first year of life (Hoffman, 1975; Ungerer et al, 1990), and that personal distress results in attempts to self-soothe be-cause the child has no sense of others at this stage of develop-ment and simply responds to arousal with self-focused behavior.

At Hoffman's (1987) second stage, the child is developing the ability to distinguish self from others and, therefore, can respond to the distress of another with appropriate affect and focus. When they understand that they themselves are not distressed, a child can maintain attention on the other individual. A child in this still immature stage of differentiation of self and others may attempt to soothe the distressed person but remains somewhat self-focused. In this stage the child's attempts to soothe will match methods previously used to soothe him or herself. Hoffman (1987) reports that a child in this stage may bring his or her own mother to soothe the distressed child even though the distressed child's mother is also present. He suggests that the level of ability to distinguish self from others is present in chil-dren at around 18 months of age.

The third stage in Hoffman's model begins around 2 to 3 years of age. At this age Hoffman suggests that children gain awareness that others have feelings and internal states independent of their own. This increasingly complex ability to take the perspective of others means that a child at this stage of development can be em-pathic to the distress of others, given enough information, even when the distressed person is not present.

Finally, in Hoffman's fourth developmental stage, which occurs in late childhood, the child acquires awareness that others have an independent history and identity of their own. Here the child can differentiate between self and others to the point of being aware that others have a separate mind with desires, intentions, beliefs, and history, which may mean that the child can feel em-pathy for a person's continuing situation as opposed to the per-ception that distress is a momentary thing. A child in this stage can demonstrate empathy for a person's chronic state, such as poverty, disability, or other persistent difficulties. Such a child can generate theories about other persons and their situation, which influences the degree of empathic affect for the other person (Hoffman, 1987). Hoffman (1975) and others have presented evidence in support of this view of the development of empathy. However, from a developmental perspective, the question then is when does empathy stop developing?

The Development of Empathy from Childhood to Adulthood

Some researchers have reported that empathy, once formed in late childhood, remains stable for at least the first two decades of life (Davis & Franzoi, 1991; Eisenberg, Carlo, Murphy, & Van Court, 1995) and Eisenberg et al. (2002) report research showing that empathy remains stable throughout adolescence and into adulthood. However, other researchers point to the modifiability of empathy with intervention well into adulthood (Lesh, 1970; Marshall, O'Sullivan, & Fernandez, 1996). This lack of agreement on the stability of empathy suggests that once fully developed, empathy will remain constant unless there is a significant event or influence that results in a reformulation of empathy for the individual. This is reflective of a dynamic systems theory approach to development, which has been used to describe differences in the development of locomotor abilities (such as walking) and attachment (for a review of dynamic systems theory approach to development see Thelen, 1995).

EMPATHY AND RELATED CONSTRUCTS

We have seen that empathy begins with innate abilities and develops through socialization to become a complex cognitive skill. As a consequence, environment seems to play an important role. There are a number of researchers who have reported an influence of environmental factors on the development of empathy. Parental attentiveness (Abraham, Kuehl, & Christopherson, 1983; Bernadett-Shapiro, Ehrensaft, & Shapiro, 1996; Frank & Hoffman, 1986; Robinson, Zahn-Waxler, & Emde, 2001; Trommsdorff, 1991), disciplinary punishment (Lopez, Bonenberger, & Schneider, 2001; Roe, 1980), and congenital and acquired deafness (Bachara, Raphael, & Phelen, 1980) have all been reported to impact empathy in predictable ways. Social competence (Adams, Schvaneveldt, & Jenson, 1979) has also been shown to be related to empathy in school-age children.

Two other areas related to socialization that could reasonably be expected to affect the development of empathy are gender and early interpersonal relationships. It has been suggested that girls are socialized to be more affective and more aware of the affect of others than are boys (Dunn, Bretherton, & Munn, 1987; Hoffman, 1977). Therefore, we may expect girls to also be more empathic than boys. Additionally, it has been theorized that the mother-infant bond forms the secure base from which infants can explore their world and is the template for future relationships (Ainsworth, 1963). Consequently, we might expect infants with insecure attachments to their primary caregivers to have difficulties in interpersonal relations with empathy being one reflection of the quality of an interpersonal relationship (Eisenberg & Strayer, 1987).

Gender Differences

Because girls and boys are socialized differently, it would be reasonable to expect differences in empathy between genders (Eisenberg, Fabes, Schaller, & Miller, 1990). Unfortunately, as with much of the research on empathy, the literature on gender differences suffers from limitations due to variations in the definitions of empathy, sympathy, personal distress, and emotional contagion (Eisenberg et al., 1990). Despite these problems, however, the results of research on gender differences have been fairly consistent with females being consistently more empathic than males (Adams, Schvaneveldt, & Jenson, 1979; Hoffman, 1977; Strayer & Roberts, 1997) and with differences between genders increasing with age (Davis, 1983; Eisenberg, Fabes, Schaller, & Miller, 1990; Eisenberg McCreath, & Ahn, 1988; Eisenberg, Shell, Pasternack, & Lennon, 1987; Feshbach & Feshbach, 1969; Litvak-Miller, McDougall, & Romney, 1997; Lopez, Bonenberger, & Schneider, 2001; Strayer & Roberts, 1997).

Empathy and Attachment

Attachment theory describes the propensity of humans to make strong affectionate bonds with others and explains the emotional distress caused by unwanted loss or separation (Bowlby, 1976). Attachment behavior describes the behavior of an individual in relation to an attachment figure. Attachment behavior in infants consists of proximity-seeking when under stress and exploratory behavior from a secure base (usually the mother) while not under stress (Ainsworth, 1963). Bell and Ainsworth (1972) report that the attachment system and the exploratory system are in dynamic equilibrium and that it is an imbalance of these two systems that leads to insecure attachment. The infant's first social relationship with the primary caregiver, usually the mother, is said to form a template for future relationships that stays with the individual from the cradle to the grave (Bowlby, 1976). Research on the influence of attachment in infancy on future behavior suggests that insecure infant-mother attachment is consistently related to more negative social outcomes. For example, the quality of attachment in infancy has been related to social-behavioral problems in early school-aged children (Goldberg, 1991; Sroufe, Egeland, & Kreutzer, 1990) and adulthood (Smallbone & Dadds, 2000). Bowlby (1969; 1973;1980) also pointed to the important role of parent/child bonds for the healthful development of the child. He observed that children with poor parent/child relationships become anxious, angry, or depressed. Subsequent research has demonstrated quite clearly that all manner of problems result from inadequate parenting (e.g., Bretherton, 1985; Loeber, 1990). Clearly, then, the quality of the infant's attachment could impact the degree and type of empathic responding.

Given that attachment patterns are hypothesized to precede the full development of empathy, and keeping in mind the importance of socialization to the development of empathy, there is surprisingly little research on attachment and empathy. However, links between attachment style and degree and type of empathic responding have been demonstrated. Insecurely attached children display less empathic responding and more personal distress type of affective responding than do children classified as securely attached (e.g., Bischof-Koehler, 2000; Kestenbaum, Farber, & Sroufe, 1989). However, the full nature of the relationship between the development of empathy and attachment style has yet to be explored and presents an interesting issue that will hopefully be examined in future research.

Conclusions

There are a number of other areas of research that have some relevance for the development of empathy. For example, studies on twins (see Zhan-Waxler, Schiro, Robinson, Emde, & Schmitz, 2001), self-regulation (see Ungerer et al., 1990; Zahn-Waxler, Robinson, & Emde, 1992), differences between empathic affect in humans for humans versus animals (Paul, 2000), and theoretically-related constructs (such as Theory of Mind, see Ward, Keenan, & Hudson, 2000) that have not been given attention in this paper. While important to the full understanding of the development of empathy, results from these research areas contribute little more to our understanding of empathy development than those covered in this chapter. Additionally, many of these areas have yet to receive extensive empirical attention. The focus here has been on the early developmental milestones that have been well documented and most strongly relate to the development of empathy.

The inescapable conclusion from a review of the literature on the development of empathy is that a comprehensive, coherent, and widely accepted definition is direly needed. A glaring example of this problem is that most of the literature on the development of empathy, despite spanning more than one hundred years, begins with each author's justification for their own idiosyncratic definition of empathy. The differentiations between constructs (e.g., empathy and sympathy and personal distress and emotional contagion) that have been outlined in this chapter are not agreed upon by all who conduct research on the development of empathy. However, most do seem to agree that there is a difference between empathy and sympathy, and each author seems to have a different explanation of the differences.

W. L. Marshall's model of empathy was examined in relation to the development of empathy. We found evidence supporting the idea that children develop the abilities Marshall describes as necessary for empathy in a fashion that parallels the increasing complexity of his model. Children, for example, seem to develop the perceptual abilities necessary to recognize the distress of others, first followed by acquisition and development of perspective taking ability. The one component of Marshall's model that violates a developmental view of empathy is that the physical ability to ameliorate the distress of others appears to develop prior to the cognitive skill necessary to take another person's perspective. It should be noted that Marshall's model was not intended to account for the development of empathy. Rather, it was meant to describe the sequential steps to empathic responding, and nothing from this review of the development of empathy counters this perspective.

Based on this review, it seems that empathy has survival utility, and at least some of its components have an innate basis. However, the development of empathy is clearly influenced by the environment. The importance of social interaction, that was illustrated by Monty Python's description of the meaning of life, was meant to describe the importance of appropriate affective functioning within a social group. Empathy, this review suggests, is comprised of a complex set of perceptual and cognitive skills and has developed as a way to aid functioning within a social group.

This chapter shows that although empathy has its roots in inherited abilities, it is socialization and the influence of other features of the environment that ultimately determine the development of empathy in an individual over one's lifespan. Evidence from research on gender differences, attachment, and interpersonal relationships supports the importance of socialization on the development of empathy. Accepting that empathy can be affected by the environment encourages us to believe that empathy can be modified in those who are deficient. Although the evidence is limited, what research is available supports the idea that empathy is modifiable well into adulthood.

4

Empathy, Social Intelligence, & Agressive Behavior

H. Moulden & W. L. Marshall

"Intelligence alone, without widsom and empathy for suffering, is hollow."
John G. Stoessinger (1927-)

In a recent seminal paper, Bjorkqvist, Osterman, and Kaukiainen (2000) proposed that social intelligence in the absence of empathy could lead to aggression. They backed up their claim by reviewing a considerable body of literature, much of it produced by themselves and their colleagues in their evaluation of various factors that generate aggression. They have examined aggression in boys and girls (Bjorkqvist, Lagerspetz, & Kaukiainen, 1992; Lagerspetz, Bjorkqvist, & Peltonen, 1988), in adult males (Bjorkqvist, Osterman, & Lagerspetz, 1994), and in adult females (Bjorkqvist & Niemela, 1992). The observations of Bjorkqvist and his colleagues represent a new way of looking at aggression. It seemed to us that their view has relevance for understanding sexual offending since it is also a form of aggression, and we know that a lack of empathy (at least in some form) characterizes sexual offenders. The intent of this chapter is to apply Bjorkqvist's model to sexual offending and make suggestions for both clinical work and research. We believe Bjorkqvist's model also has relevance not only for other forms of overt aggression but also for covert aggression and for passive-aggressive behaviors. First we will attempt to clarify the meaning of social intelligence, then we will describe empathy as it might fit into this model, and finally we will integrate these two notions as suggested by Bjorkqvist et al.

SOCIAL INTELLIGENCE

The evolution of intelligence shows an increase in flexibility and complexity with the appearance of new animal species throughout the long history of life, reaching its pinnacle among land animals in the primates. Most of the great apes are social animals and Humphrey (1976) has, accordingly, argued for a social origin for primate intelligence. He points out that chimpanzees, for example, are clearly quite intelligent animals, and yet their life as foragers does not seem to demand anything like that level of intelligence. It is, so Humphrey says, the demands of their complex social life that require this. Humans have even more complex social lives with social interaction relying heavily on the use of language. Thus quite intricate skills and marked flexibility are required to function effectively within these complicated interactive systems. We live in groups, and this requires us to elicit the cooperation of others in order to achieve our goals. As Goody notes, this means humans must "be calculating beings; they must be able to calculate the consequences of their own behavior, to calculate the likely behavior of others, to calculate the balance of the advantage and loss—and all this in a context where the evidence on which their calculations are based is ephemeral, ambiguous, and liable to change, not least as a consequence of their own action" (Goody, 1995, p.2).

From this general perspective, intelligence is said to have rapidly evolved among hominids and their closely related cousins the chimpanzees, bonobos, and gorillas as a result of pressures to maximize social effectiveness and, consequently, survival. Thus, social intelligence (or intelligence in the service of socially-mediated goals, for example, sex) is seen as the generic intelligence from which academic intelligence (i.e., what psychologists typically think of as "real" intelligence) is an accidental spin-off. Not surprisingly, this view has critics (Glasser & Zimmerman, 1967; Wechsler, 1958). Of course social and academic intelligence do not exhaust all possible forms of, or applications of, intelligence. Gardner (1983), for example, listed six "compartmentalized intelligences": linguistic, logico-mathematical, spatial, musical, kinaesthetic, and personal intelligence. The first three are typically assessed in tests of general intelligence (Wechsler, 1958), whereas the last-mentioned corresponds with what has been called either social intelligence or interactive intelligence (Levinson, 1995).

The concept of intelligence has a long history, but the first attempts to convert this concept into a measure that might be used to assess people occurred in the latter part of the nineteenth century (Binet & Simon, 1905; Galton, 1869) and the early part of the twentieth century (Spearman, 1927; Thurstone, 1938). Intelligence, as defined by these early researchers and by most who have followed them (e.g., Wechsler, 1958), was restricted to those skills thought necessary to excel at academic pursuits. Thorndike, one of the great early American psychologists, appears to have been the first to suggest that social intelligence was one aspect of intelligent behavior that was separate from these academic skills. He (Thorndike, 1920) described social intelligence as "...the ability to understand and manage men and women, boys and girls–to act wisely in human relations" (p. 228).

These abilities, Thorndike thought, allowed people to understand others and to act wisely toward them. Thus, he saw social intelligence as similar to what we would describe today as social or interpersonal skills. Thorndike's ideas were greeted with enthusiasm by various psychologists, and there followed several attempts to convert Thorndike's concept into workable measures for assessing social intelligence. In what appears to be the first such attempt, Moss, Hunt, Omwake and Ronning (1927) described the George Washington University Test of Social Intelligence. This measure included features such as (1) judgements of social situations, (2) memory for faces and names, (3) observations of the behavior of others, (4) recognition of emotional states in others, (5) recognition of the meaning of facial expressions, and (6) questions of social interest.

Hunt (1928) somewhat broadened Thorndike's notion to include a person's general ability to accurately judge social situations and to deal effectively with people. In fact, Hunt declared that "judgement in social situations is almost an infallible indication of social intelligence" (Hunt, 1928, p. 321). Although Chapin (1939) attempted to develop a measure of social insight, his measure only assessed the person's capacity to understand themselves. This represented a marked shift away from a concern with judgements about others and about social situations to more intrapersonal processes. No doubt Chapin's concept of what might be called personal intelligence (or self-insight) is a useful one deserving of both clinical and research attention, and it was taken up much later by Wedeck (1947). Wedeck suggested that what he called "psychological ability" was the capacity to develop personal insight. He proposed that once an individual had insight into his/her own cognitions, behaviors, and emotions, then he/she would be able to perceive more accurately these experiences in others. Nevertheless, these notions do not fit with what most writers have considered social intelligence; although, as Wedeck suggested, greater self-insight likely enhances the capacity to accurately perceive others.

Vernon, another of the great early American psychologists, became interested in social intelligence. He expanded Thorndike's ideas to define social intelligence as "the ability to get along with people in general, social technique, or ease in society, knowledge of social matters, susceptibility to stimuli from others... as well as insight into the temporary moods or the underlying personality traits of friends or strangers" (Vernon, 1933, p. 44). Judgements of personality were most prominent in Vernon's concept, and, not surprisingly, personality ratings formed an important aspect of his measures of social intelligence. This, however, like Chapin's measures, taps only one aspect of what is usually meant by social intelligence.

According to Walker and Foley's (1973) comprehensive review, a divide emerged between those studying social intelligence and those interested in the accuracy of interpersonal judgements. Their review also revealed a lack of agreement on the definition of social intelligence and, as a consequence, no agreement at all on what constituted an appropriate measure of the concept. What were clearly aspects of social intelligence by some were considered to be distinct domains of functioning by others. For example, research on role-taking, interpersonal skills, social judgements, and empathy was typically conducted with little or no mention of their role in social intelligence. This confusion, which had characterized the field since its earliest days, led to a lessening of interest in social intelligence from the 1940s to the late 1960s.

When interest resurfaced, there was a shift in approach. Of particular relevance was the emergence of a focus on interpersonal competence (Weinstein, 1969). Interpersonal competence, as defined by Weinstein involved "the ability to accomplish interpersonal tasks (and) the ability to manipulate others" (Weinstein, 1969, p. 755). He claimed that if a person could take the perspective of someone else, then they would be more likely to accurately predict the other person's behavior. They would, thereby, be better able to anticipate the responses of others and, as a result, exercise greater control over social interactions. If social intelligence is to be a meaningful concept, then clearly the ability to accurately perceive the emotions and thoughts of others is crucial to the definition.

Keating (1978) attempted to address the confusion in the field that had led to diminished interest. His reading of the literature led him to suggest there were three important questions the field needed to address: (1) is social intelligence a separate and unitary factor? (2) can measures of social intelligence predict social maturity and social functioning? and (3) are scores on various measures of social intelligence more related to each other than to measures of other constructs (e.g., general intelligence)? On the latter issue, Glasser and Zimmerman (1967) and Wechsler (1958) both claimed that social intelligence was simply the application of general intelligence to social situations. This claim seems to run counter to everyday experience, which suggests that some academically bright people function quite poorly socially while some socially skilled people are poor at academic work. However, Keating found evidence that scores on measures of social intelligence were as strongly correlated with scores on academic performance as they were with each other. He also showed that social intelligence was not a single and unitary factor, and measures of social intelligence did not predict behavior. He concluded that at that time, validation of social intelligence was difficult due to the nature of the competing and inadequate definitions and the poor measures available. Walker and Foley's (1973) earlier review came to similar dismal conclusions.

In response to these gloomy conclusions, Ford and Tisak (1983) pointed out that measures of social intelligence had rested on paper-and-pencil tests. These tests essentially asked questions about abstract situations and allowed the respondents to portray themselves as perhaps more effective than they were. They suggested that since social intelligence is manifested in behavior, measures should tap actual behavior rather than ask for reports about what people think they can or might do. Perhaps more importantly, actual behavior catches the dynamics crucial to social intelligence, which cannot be captured by self-report measures.

First, however, it is necessary to be really clear about what social intelligence is.

Social intelligence concerns the idea that the basis for effective social functioning rests on a specific form of intelligence that governs how well people are able to monitor their own behavior and that of others, predict the consequences of their behavior on others, predict the responses of others, and modulate their own behavior accordingly. Accurate analysis of the reciprocal aspects of social functioning is essential to meeting needs that are mediated socially. Anthropological researchers have cast this skill in terms of what they call "anticipatory interactive planning" (Goody, 1995). Social intelligence, construed in this manner, carries no implications of moral behavior. Intimidation or manipulation may work as effectively to achieve a person's goals as would more kindly behavior. Such manipulative behaviors may manifest as either a persistent style, or they may only be evident in specific circumstances.

The literature on psychopaths suggests they can read other people's responses sufficiently well to get what they want (Marshall & Barbaree, 1984). Psychopaths modulate their own behavior such that they can either manipulate others to do what they want or intimidate them to get the cooperation they need (Marshall & Serin, 1997). Being able to read others well and modify responding accordingly are two of the cardinal features of social intelligence, and psychopaths are clearly able to do both well, yet they still hurt others. Even otherwise prosocial people who are highly socially intelligent will occasionally abuse the rights of others or even aggress against them (Felson, 2000). In fact, Batson and his colleagues have shown that a substantial number of normal people, when faced with the suffering of another person, will attempt to escape from the situation rather than help the person who is suffering (Batson, Duncan, Ackerman, Buckley, & Birch, 1981; Batson, O'Quin, Fultz, Vanderplas, & Isen, 1983; Toi & Batson, 1982). Thus being socially intelligent is not synonymous with being prosocial. In fact, as a result of their studies of apes, who are seen to have primarily selfish goals, social anthropologists have described apes' social intelligence as Machiavellian (Byrne, 1995) precisely because the intentions of such behaviors are not prosocial. In attempting to make sense of these observations, Bjorkqvist, Osterman and Kaukiainen (2000) suggested that in the absence of empathy, social intelligence can readily lead to aggression. This notion of Bjorkqvist et al. provides the basis of the present chapter.

In attempting to formulate behavioral criteria that can serve as a measure of social intelligence, we need to be concerned about features that are components of other skills, some of which may be independent of social intelligence while others may overlap with social intelligence. The more our measures tap social intelligence alone, the more meaningful the results will be. For example, the ability to accurately decode the nonverbal cues and behaviors of other people would appear to be an integral component of social intelligence. Sternberg and Smith (1985) examined this issue but could not find any evidence that decoding skills were related to scores on measures of social intelligence. Barnes and Sternberg (1989) suggest that in testing decoding ability, there may be a number of skills involved, only some of which are related to social intelligence. This, they suggested, might account for Sternberg and Smith's failure to find a relationship. In their research, Barnes and Sternberg (1989) did find that decoding ability was related both to self-reported social competence and to scores on a number of tests of social intelligence. They concluded that these findings were due to the fact that both social intelligence and decoding share underlying skills involved in the ability to create effective strategies when examining people for social information (such as facial cues) and to utilize this information to govern actions. Thus some aspects of decoding skills are fundamental to social intelligence.

It is apparent that a variety of skills are involved in functioning as a socially intelligent person, but are all these skills part of social intelligence, and are they involved in related behaviors? Although Ford and Tisak (1983) generated evidence suggesting that social intelligence is a unitary construct distinct from other skills such as academic intelligence, their findings did not exclude the possibility that social intelligence is multidimensional. Marlowe (1986) asked what domains are associated with social intelligence. Using a variety of tools to measure social interests, social self-efficacy, empathy skills, interpersonal behavioral skills, and general intelligence, Marlowe concluded that social intelligence involved five domains of functioning. He suggested the following domains should be assessed in measures of social intelligence: social attitudes, interpersonal skills, empathy skills, emotionality, and social ease/anxiety. Consistent with previous research, Marlowe showed that social intelligence was independent of academic intelligence, a finding that continues to be supported in recent research (Campbell & McCord, 1996).

Despite Marlowe's findings, it is possible to construe social intelligence as independent of empathy skills, and it is not entirely clear why emotionality and social ease/anxiety should be seen as part of the definition. What we need to ask is what are the necessary and sufficient set of behaviors that generate effective social intelligence? Of course, to do this we need a measure of the product of using social intelligence, that is, what it is we expect the exercise of social intelligence to produce. Presumably, achieving one's goals at low cost would be one measure of the effectiveness of social intelligence; although, even effective behavior does not always produce the desired result. Certainly, generally effective social functioning would be expected to provide an index of social intelligence, and essentially this is the basis of the measure developed by Kaukianinen, Bjorkqvist, Osterman, Lagerspetz, and Forsblom (1995) for use with school children. Their Peer-Estimated Social Intelligence (PESI) requires children familiar with the target child to estimate the target child's social intelligence on a number of observable behavioral features. Kaukiainen et al. have shown this measure to be reliable and valid, and they and their colleagues have used it in a series of studies. We (Moulden & Marshall, 2002) have recently adapted this measure for use with adults, and we are in the process of collecting psychometric data, which hopefully will support the use of this adaptation.

For the purposes of this writing, social intelligence is defined as the ability to achieve personally defined goals within a social context. This requires us to clearly recognize our own goals and motivations, to formulate plans to achieve them, to recognize the constraints imposed by both circumstances and the needs of the other persons present, to read other people's emotions and predict their likely responses to our behavior, and to modulate our behavior accordingly. In this sense, social intelligence plays a role in all social interactions, both those with prosocial and antisocial outcomes. A highly socially intelligent person will likely prefer prosocial ways of meeting his/her goals, but such an astute person may also conclude, perhaps only on occasion, that the only way to achieve his/her goal is through the use of some form of aggression, even if it is only indirect (e.g., manipulating, ignoring, or excluding the other person).

Empathy and Social Intelligence

Definitions of empathy have, until recently, been varied with little agreement across researchers. The study of empathy has followed two distinct paths based on two definitions or conceptualizations of the empathic process. Following Dymond's (1949) cognitive-role-taking approach, some theorists have defined empathy in terms of accurately predicting another person's thoughts and feelings (Cline & Richards, 1960; Dymond, 1950). An alternative approach has concentrated on the experience of a vicarious emotional response (Stotland, 1969; Eisenberg, 1986; Moore, 1990). Current definitions of empathy consider both cognitive and emotional aspects including both the ability to recognize another person's emotion as well as the observer's response to that recognition (Davis, 1983; Eisenberg & Miller, 1987; Marshall, Hudson, Jones, & Fernandez, 1995). Marshall et al. (1995), for example, formulated a four-stage model of empathy involving emotional recognition, perspective-taking, experiencing a compassionate emotional response, and taking action to comfort or reduce suffering.

When we consider the definitions of social intelligence outlined in the previous section, we can see that the first two stages of Marshall et al.'s model match aspects of these definitions. Social intelligence requires the person to be adept at recognizing emotional responses in others and to be good at seeing things from the other person's perspective. In fact, Vernon (1933), in his definition of social intelligence included "insight into the states of and traits of others." Another social intelligence pioneer, Wedeck (1947), expanded his idea to include the ability to judge other people accurately. Also, Goody's (1995) definition of anticipatory interactive planning (her descriptor for social intelligence) clearly relies on the person's ability to accurately perceive the emotions, thoughts, and likely the actions of others. Thus, although until recently empathy and social intelligence have been studied separately, it is clear there is considerable overlap in the processes recognized as critical to both. Even somewhat recent studies have employed a measure of empathy as one of various tests used to assess social intelligence (Ford, 1982; Ford & Tisak, 1983; Marlowe, 1986). Ford and Tisak (1983), for example, include Hogan's (1969) Empathy Scale and The Empathy Test (Kerr & Speroff, 1947) as part of their measure of social intelligence. The important question then becomes "Is empathy part of social intelligence or are they overlapping constructs?" One way to better understand their relationship and how they influence behavior is to conceptualize and operationalize them as unique and distinct constructs. This is what Bjorkqvist et al. (2000) have done, and this is a course we hope to follow.

Empathy has been clearly implicated in the mediation of behavior, both antisocial and prosocial behavior (Feshbach, 1987; Moore, 1990). Moore (1990), for example, has proposed that empathy plays a necessary role in altruistic behavior such that the altruistic person must be empathic in order to be motivated to self-sacrifice. He says that in order to act altruistically, a person must have an emotional frame of reference to which he/she can compare the reactions of the other person. This comparative emotional reference would then trigger the altruistic actions. As we will see, empathy can serve either to inhibit the initiation of aggressive behavior or curtail ongoing aggression (Miller & Eisenberg, 1988). Empathy, then, can initiate a general concern for others that might trigger self-sacrifice in the assistance (compassionate behavior) or protection of others (altruism) as well as prevent us from doing harm to others.

Although empathy relies on processes such as emotional recognition and perspective-taking, which are also components of social intelligence, it also involves the initiation of a feeling state in the observer (either a feeling of compassion or a shared feeling of distress) and an active response by the observer to ameliorate the distress of the target person. In addition, social intelligence has other components (e.g., accurate anticipation of the other person's reactions) and also serves other purposes (e.g., the achievement of socially mediated personal goals). For example, Thorndike's (1920) definition considered the ability to manage others to be an important aspect of social intelligence, and Weinstein's (1969) conceptualization of interpersonal competence emphasized the importance of perspective-taking for the purpose of controlling others. It is, therefore, conceptually possible to distinguish these two constructs, social intelligence and empathy, in ways that would allow us to evaluate their separate contributions to behavior.

Based on the information we gather interpersonally in our every-day lives, we all make choices about how to react. We may choose to react either positively or negatively, but, in either case, that choice is based on social cues and knowledge, that is, on social intelligence. If we look at aggressive behavior as an example from the antisocial response set, we have an opportunity to examine the differential paths that the relationship between empathy and social intelligence may take in terms of both prosocial and antisocial interactions.

EMPATHY, SOCIAL INTELLIGENCE, AND AGGRESSION

In a meta-analysis that integrated evidence from a variety of studies, Miller and Eisenberg (1988) concluded that empathy can inhibit aggressive behavior (see also Richardson, Hammock, Smith, Gardner, & Signo, 1994). These authors suggested that when aggression does occur, it results from a failure to be inhibited because there is an absence of an empathic response to the victim's distress. Given empathy's well-established role as a mediator of behavior (Feshbach, 1987; Moore, 1990), if the aggressor could recognize the distress of the victim and experience a compassionate response, this should reduce the inclination to continue to aggress (Miller & Eisenberg, 1988). Consistent with this, there is evidence suggesting that empathy training is successful in reducing the incidence of subsequent aggressive behavior (Feshbach, 1989; Kalliopuska & Tiitinen, 1991). Given this evidence, there is practical importance in attempting to further study the role of both empathy and social intelligence in interpersonal aggression.

As suggested in our consideration of social intelligence, it is related to the expression of both prosocial and antisocial behaviors.

After reviewing the state of social intelligence research, Walker and Foley (1973) challenged researchers to address the issue concerning those people who know what behavior should be exhibited because they are capable of "reading social cues" (p. 847) but choose not to act prosocially. This challenge has been, and continues to be, comprehensively addressed in the work of Bjorkqvist and his colleagues in Finland. They have completed a series of important studies addressing aggression and a number of mitigating factors such as gender, age, culture, and more recently, empathy and social intelligence. Their research has focused primarily on children who engage in aggressive or bullying behavior. Of course, empathy, social intelligence, and aggression are also found in adults, and presumably similar results should be obtained with them as with children.

Because self-reports of empathy, social intelligence, and aggression are influenced by the desire to appear socially appropriate, such measures may provide misleading data. In response to this problem, Bjorkqvist and his colleagues designed measures that are based on peer-estimations. Although such measures have received some criticism (Ford & Tisak, 1983; Cossio, Hernandez-Guzman, & Lopez, 2000), they are still considered superior to paper-and-pencil tests.

The work of Bjorkqvist and his colleagues, based on the use of peer-estimates of actual behavior, has contributed significantly to our understanding of childhood aggression and needs to be expanded to include adults. Examining the relationship between empathy and social intelligence in terms of their influence on aggressive behavior should ultimately provide information relevant to treating aggressive people. In order to effectively examine the relationships between these two processes (i.e., empathy and social intelligence) and aggression, we need to consider in more detail the nature of aggression.

Aggression

Researchers have distinguished three categories of aggressive behavior: indirect, verbal, and physical aggression (Baron & Richardson, 1994). For many years, physical attacks were the sole focus of aggression research. Although this approach neglected other forms of aggression, it was appropriate initially since the primary subjects were animals or small children. These subjects obviously either lacked (or had limited) verbal skills, and as a consequence, they relied on physical means to aggress. As the verbal skills of humans develop with increasing age, they become additional tools for aggression, and, accordingly, the working definition of aggression has to be expanded. The available research on the development of aggressive behaviors (Bjorkqvist, Lagerspetz, & Kaukiainen, 1992; Bjorkqvist, Osterman, & Kaukiainen, 1992) reveals that as social skills develop, more sophisticated means of aggression become available. Such sophistication even allows the aggressor to target a victim without being identified. Indirect aggression, as this is called, takes the form of acts such as manipulation or exclusion from a desired social group (Bjorkqvist, Osterman, & Kaukiainen, 1992).

Based on definitions of aggression in simply verbal or physical terms, it was concluded that boys are more aggressive than girls (Maccoby & Jacklin, 1974). When indirect aggression was included, the results changed. Among children, indirect aggression is more prevalent in girls than in boys and begins to emerge around age eleven years (Feshbach, 1969; Lagerspetz, Bjorkqvist & Peltonen,1988). When a definition of aggression was used that included all possible forms of expression (verbal, physical, and indirect), fewer differences between genders were apparent, and those differences were more qualitative than quantitiative (Lagerspetz, Bjorkqvist et al., 1988; Bjorkqvist, Osterman, & Kaukiainen, 1992). However, with age, the qualitative differences also decreased.

Aggression does not necessarily diminish once adulthood is reached (Feshbach, 1970; Bjorkqvist & Niemela, 1992), but rather the methods of expressing aggression become more covert and less recognizable (Bjorkqvist, Osterman, & Lagerspetz, 1994). Interestingly, in their research on the developmental course of aggression, Bjorkqvist, Osterman, and Lagerspetz (1994) found that covert (i.e., indirect) aggression was used equally by both men and women; although, they differed in their preferred style (Bjorkqvist, Osterman, & Hjelt-Back, 1994; Bjorkqvist, Osterman, & Lagerspetz, 1994). Men were found more likely than women to use a subtype of covert aggression called rational-appearing aggression, whereas women used a different subtype called social manipulation more often. An example of rational-appearing aggression is the use of nonconstructive criticism, whereas social manipulation involves, for example, getting others to facilitate the exclusion of the victim from a desired group (Bjorkqvist, Osterman, & Lagerspetz, 1994).

The Role of Social Intelligence & Empathy on Aggressive Displays

Bjorkqvist, Osterman, and Kaukiainen, (2000) describe social intelligence as having a perceptual, a cognitive analytical, and a behavioral (skills) component. They say the "socially intelligent individual is capable of producing adequate behavior for the purpose of achieving desired social goals" (Bjorkqvist, Osterman, & Kaukiainen, 2000, p. 192). As we have seen, social intelligence is involved in all types of behavior and is particularly important when it comes to choosing and enacting behaviors in a given social situation. Social intelligence helps us decide which response set is likely to be appropriate (i.e., have the maximum benefits and the least costs) for the emotional climate of the interaction. In times of conflict, social intelligence is an asset in that it provides the individual with the skills to achieve resolution and the option to do so peacefully. However, such astute analyses of others also allows the person to accurately select one or another form of aggression to terminate conflict and to achieve their goals without regard for the other person's needs.

In developing a theory about the relationship between empathy and social intelligence with respect to aggression, it is important to note that high levels of social intelligence are particularly important in indirect aggression. This is because the sophisticated perpetrator has the skills necessary to harm the victim by means of social manipulation (i.e., circuitously rather than directly) and, as a result, to protect himself/herself from potential retaliation (Bjorkqvist, Osterman, & Kaukiainen, 2000). It could, therefore, be predicted that social intelligence will be more highly correlated with indirect forms of aggression than with either verbal or physical aggression.

Kaukiainen and his colleagues (Kaukiainen et al., 1999; Kaukiainen, Bjorkqvist, Osterman, Lagerspetz, & Niskanen, 1994; Kaukiainen, Bjorkqvist, Osterman, & Lagerspetz, 1996) examined the relationship between social intelligence, empathy, and aggressive behavior. Social intelligence was most strongly positively related to the expression of indirect aggression, whereas empathy mitigated the expression of all forms of aggression. A more comprehensive study reported in Bjorkqvist, Osterman and Kaukiainen (2000) found that the significant relationships observed in children between social intelligence and the three forms of aggression were all significantly increased when the influence of empathy was removed from the correlations. Thus empathy served to attenuate each form of aggression; although, the effects of both social intelligence and empathy were most marked in indirect forms of aggression. Interestingly, the strong relationship observed between social intelligence and what Bjorkqvist et al. called "peaceful conflict resolution," was reduced when empathy was removed from the correlation. This means that the combination of high levels of social intelligence and high levels of empathy increased the likelihood that conflict would be settled in a peaceful way. Not surprisingly, empathy was strongly correlated ($r = .80$ $p<.001$) with this peaceful outcome. Another observation of Bjorkqvist et al. worth noting concerns the fact that the weakest relationship between social intelligence and aggressive behavior was with physical aggression ($r = .22$, $p<.05$). Indeed the magnitude of the correlations between social intelligence and the different forms of behavior studied by Bjorkqvist and his colleagues decreased in a step-wise manner from a peaceful resolution ($r =.80$) to indirect aggression ($r =.55$), to verbal aggression ($r =.30$), and finally to physical aggression.

In the summary of their excellent and provocative paper, Bjorkqvist et al. (2000) conclude that social intelligence is needed for all forms of aggression and also for peaceful solutions to problems. The fact that the strength of the relationship between social intelligence and responses to conflict is ordered according to how wise the behaviors are (i.e., from peaceful solutions to indirect aggression, to verbal aggression, and to physical aggression) "suggests that socially intelligent individuals choose methods that expose them to as little danger as possible" (Bjorkqvist et al., 2000, p. 197). Nevertheless, the fact remains that social intelligence is related even to physical aggression whereas empathy is unrelated to this form of conflict resolution ($r = -.04$). Socially intelligent people clearly sometimes resort to physical aggression, but when they do, it is either because they lack empathy, or, more likely, because they simply lose or give up their capacity to be empathic toward the other person, perhaps as a result of the conflict.

Conclusions

Social intelligence appears to be involved in the entire spectrum of behaviors required for effective interpersonal communication. Until recently, social intelligence was conceptualized most often in terms of its role in prosocial interactions, and, in fact, prosocial behavior has been included as a component in defining social intelligence (Marlowe, 1986). Unfortunately, social intelligence also plays a role in antisocial behavior. Not only is it related to aggressive behavior, but the strength of that relationship depends on the form of aggression used. If social intelligence is related to both prosocial and antisocial behaviors, there must be a third factor mediating this relationship. Empathy has been proposed as an inhibitor of aggressive behavior, and research findings concur with this proposal. Therefore, it should not be surprising that, as we have found, social intelligence in someone who is capable of feeling empathy results in prosocial interactions, even in the face of conflict, whereas social intelligence without empathy results in some form of aggression. Lower levels of social intelligence are related to more physical demonstrations of aggression, whereas higher levels of social intelligence are involved in more indirect forms such as social manipulation.

Since empathy attenuates all forms of aggression, it seems logical to propose that training clients (who aggress) to be more empathic will contribute to a future reduction in their propensity to aggress. For some clients, it may be necessary to increase their general disposition to be empathic, but for others, their apparent lack of empathy may be specific to the particular victim or to the set of circumstances that are consistently present at the time of their aggressive acts. For example, among sexual offenders, we have found that the majority do not lack empathy toward most people but do lack empathy toward their victims (Fernandez & Marshall, in press; Fernandez, Marshall, Lightbody, & O'Sullivan, 1999). This apparent lack of empathy toward their victims appears to result from various rationalizations and justifications they use to either disregard the victim's feelings or to enable them to ignore the victim's distress. We have developed effective strategies to enhance victim empathy in sexual offenders (Marshall & Fernandez, 2001; Marshall, O'Sullivan, & Fernandez, 1996) as have others (Hildebran & Pithers, 1989; Pithers, 1994).

This review of the evidence suggests that training subjects in the skills necessary to achieve high levels of social intelligence should reduce the tendency to aggress. These reductions in apparent aggression, however, may simply mask a shift from overt (i.e., physical or verbal) aggression to more covert forms (e.g., manipulation) unless empathy is also enhanced. Increases in social intelligence should be readily attainable since the component skills of social intelligence are well defined and clearly modifiable. For example, it has been found that social cognition processes necessary for the accurate interpretation of the behavior of others are defective in aggressive children (Dodge, 1980; Huesmann, 1988). Enhancing the accuracy of social cognitions might, therefore, reduce aggression in these children. Of course, empathy enhancement may also be required. Masten et al. (1995) found that social competence protected children from becoming aggressive even when they were exposed to known risk factors, and various other researchers (Cowan, Wyman, Work, & Parker, 1990; Dubow & Tisak, 1989; Rutter, 1990; Werner & Smith, 1992) have found that aspects of social intelligence such as cognitive/social problem-solving skills and self-esteem also protect otherwise vulnerable children. Thus, clear targets for treatment are readily identifiable, and reasonable measures of change are available for the various features of social intelligence. These combinations of training in social intelligence skills and empathy enhancement should be major features of treatment programs for all forms of aggression; although, there are obviously other aspects to such acts that need to be addressed (Baron & Richardson, 1994; Marshall, Anderson, & Fernandez, 1999).

5

Empathy Deficits, Self-Esteem, & Cognitive Distortions in Sexual Offenders

D. Anderson & P. G. Dodgson

"By suppressing desire we try to rebuild and bolster self-esteem."
Eric Hoffer (1902-1983)

In clinical work, it can be difficult to ascertain the extent to which clients are capable of expressing genuine empathy. In their review of empathy measures, Greer, Estupinan, and Manguno-Mire (2000) noted that few studies went beyond examining the ability to recognize emotions. Perspective-taking and behavioral responses based on relevant information were virtually ignored. These authors opined that measures assessing empathy as a global trait offer little in the quest to distinguish among offenders. For the clinician who desires to assess changes in empathy levels, it appears that many measures are inadequate and may merely gauge changes in a client's vocabulary of emotions (see Chapter 2 for a discussion of the value of various measures of empathy). While the importance of being able to discern and describe emotions is noted in many definitions of empathy, changes in emotional vocabulary may not result in important changes in thinking and behavior.

Situational Influences

In addition to difficulties with measures of empathy, the context in which clients are assessed and treated may also affect their expression of empathy, both during treatment and during the course of completing assessment measures. It was noted in Chapter 1 that the emotional reaction to the perception of another person's distress may be so distressing to perceivers that they will become so focused on relieving their own distress that these perceivers will appear unempathic. It was also noted in Chapter 1 that, depending on the relationship between the perceiver and the distressed person, either pleasure at the other person's distress or empathic concern might be the resultant response. Thus the perceiver's capacity to deal with observed distress and his/her relationship with the distressed person influence whether or not empathy occurs.

In the case of sexual offenders, most enter into treatment because otherwise they face extremely negative consequences. For those who have not yet been charged with a criminal offense, they typically enter treatment hoping to avoid criminal charges and possible incarceration. Offenders who have been convicted and incarcerated are informed that the likelihood of securing any form of conditional release is markedly reduced if they do not enter into a treatment program. Incarceration is an unpleasant experience, and offenders' perception of themselves as "victims" of an "unfair system" likely mitigates against care and concern for their victims. This experience, coupled with what might be perceived by the sexual offenders as a lack of choice about entering treatment, can result in treatment resistance manifested as hostile reactions and self-pity. Certainly, these factors do not predispose clients to behave empathically.

Another related situational factor is the length of time that has passed since an offender's conviction. For those who are still "reeling" from the experience of being convicted and sentenced, they too are not likely to demonstrate much empathy for victims. Some offenders may, in fact, blame their victims for their own current situation; such feelings would clearly undermine feelings of care and concern for victims, an effect that may last for some time. If an offender's level of victim-specific empathy is being assessed shortly after his conviction, the results might indicate a lower level of empathy than might be evident at a later testing, even without the benefits of intervention.

Sexual offenders are also influenced by significant others. It is important to assess how such significant others view the offenses, the victims, and the offender's responsibility. An offender's apparent lack of victim empathy may not be surprising if his loved ones attribute responsibility for the offense to people other than the offender.

> Fred was serving a sentence of five years for sexual assaults that spanned a ten-year time period. He committed his offenses against several nieces, who at the time, ranged in age from three to ten years. After his incarceration, Fred's wife wrote a letter to the warden of the institution in an apparent effort to show support for her husband. She stated that she could tell when people were lying, and while these children may have suffered some abuse, they had embellished their stories. She added that it was the emotional vulnerability of these children that caused their abuse. She asserted that if these children had not been raised in such a poor environment, they would not have been abused, and they would be more truthful in their account of events. Nowhere in her letter did she mention her husband's responsibility for the offenses despite the fact that her own sister's children were among the victims.

As a result of his wife's position, Fred was able to distance himself from his victims' suffering and did not, as a consequence, display empathy for them. In this, and other similar cases, the offender's denial of full responsibility (and thereby avoidance of accepting he has done harm) must be maintained if he is to retain the acceptance of family members. In these cases, failure to display empathy results from a need to deny responsibility. A notion put forward by Marshall, Hudson, Jones, and Fernandez (1995) that is theoretically, in offenders who have the capacity for empathy, apparent empathy deficits may reflect cognitive distortions of the offense.

It is clear that the apparent empathy deficits seen in sexual offenders are not necessarily difficulties with empathy in general. As we have seen, these deficits may result from a denial of responsibility, but they may also be victim-specific. Indeed, there is evidence to support this possibility. When Fernandez, Marshall, Lightbody, and O'Sullivan (1996) used an empathy measure that specified different situations including people in general, victims who were sexually assaulted by someone else as well as the offender's own victim, they were able to distinguish sexual offenders from nonoffenders. Fernandez et al.'s results supported the claim of Marshall et al. (1995) that the lack of empathy observed in the sexual offenders was primarily specific to their own victims. They interpreted these results as meaning that these apparent deficits were due not to true empathy deficits but rather to the distorted ways in which these offenders perceive their victims. It was suggested that sexual offenders deliberately withhold recognition of victim harm in order to protect their sense of self-worth.

COGNITIVE DISTORTIONS IN SEXUAL OFFENDERS

"Cognitive distortions" refers to more than just denial and minimization. Attitudes, beliefs, and schemas are also usually seen as distortions and certainly other features of distorted perceptions are selective interpretation and abstraction (i.e., focusing only on,

or taking out of context, the details that fit one's assumptions);
arbitrary inferences; polarized, or dichotomous, thinking;
catastrophizing; negative attributions; erroneous assumptions
and jumping to conclusions; and emotional reasoning (for detailed explanations, refer to Beck, 1988, and Burns, 1980). For
the purposes of illustrating the concepts in this chapter, a focus
on denial and minimization of offenses will suffice.

Cognitive distortions relevant to sexual offenses are often described
in terms of denial and minimization. Cognitive distortions related
to denial frequently involve the circumstances of the offense. For
example, some offenders deny sexual interaction with certain victims. At times they will claim there was an interaction, but this interaction was not sexual in nature. Some examples of this type of
denial include the offender stating that he was giving a child victim
a bath, rubbing cream on irritated genitals, or had accidentally
brushed up against the breast of an adult female victim. They may
also claim that the victim did not resist the sexual interaction, often
stating that the victim initiated the sexual contact.

The content of cognitive distortions related to minimization is
also related to circumstances of the offense. Offenders sometimes admit to sexually assaulting the victim but admit only to
certain aspects of the offense (e.g., fondling) and not to others
(e.g., vaginal or anal intercourse). Also, offenders will frequently
admit to the sexual aspects of the offenses but not to the nonsexual physical violence, threats, or use of weapons during the
offense. Minimization can also be in the form of minimizing responsibility for the offense, attributing behavior to uncontrollable
sexual urges, a history of being victimized, or a lack of memory
for having committed the offense. Such attributions may also ex-
tend toward external circumstances such as intoxication, stress,
or peer pressure.

Eventually, many (if not most) offenders in treatment make progress with respect to their denial and minimization of offenses (Abracen, Looman, & Anderson, 2000; Barbaree, 1991) alongside progress in the area of victim awareness and empathy. Importantly, offenders are not necessarily altering their actual beliefs; they may simply change the way they disclose their own behavior and the behavior of their victims. These advances in their discussions of their offenses suggest that the offenders are initially engaging in strategies to protect themselves. Many clients have indicated they are frightened of the prospect of disclosing their sexually offending behavior in a group environment. At times, this fear actually prevents a client from even enrolling in a treatment program. As one offender in a maximum-security institution stated to the therapists, "Yeah, I'll take treatment – but I'm not talking to guys in this joint."

RELEVANCE OF SELF-ESTEEM

We (Marshall, Anderson, & Fernandez, 1999) have previously proposed that the cognitive distortions and statements suggesting a lack of empathy for victims are related to preserving self-esteem. In general, all of us engage in cognitive processes that result in self-serving biases in our interpretations of events, our behavior, or the behavior of others such that we can maintain our sense of self-worth (Blaine & Crocker, 1993). When we work with sexual offenders, we require them to discuss highly inappropriate, extremely negative and harmful behavior that they have perpetrated against others. Not only are they to talk about this behavior with us but also in the context of a group, which is usually comprised of men who are unknown to them. Furthermore, we ask them to do this after they have been through a lengthy process of being charged, convicted, and sentenced. In those contexts, they have discussed this behavior with people who they know are going to react in a hostile or negative manner (e.g., police) and with those who they fear will reject them (e.g., family members). These previous disclosures have likely been delivered in a deceitful or circuitous manner for the purpose of protecting the offender's sense of self-worth. By the time these men arrive in a treatment group, they are well-practiced in attempts to avoid negative reactions and are likely motivated to continue doing so. The offender's fear of negative evaluation is valid; after all, he has committed an offense that, in the eyes of the general public, is abhorrent. Given that offenders are more likely to perceive negative feedback from others as threatening if they also evaluate themselves negatively, those with low self-esteem can be expected to use self-serving biases in their interpretations of events because of their increased need to protect their already low sense of self-worth (Spencer, Josephs, & Steele, 1993).

As illustrative of these processes, consider the following case: Reverend A is a 32-year-old male who was referred for evaluation after an allegation of sexual abuse that occurred 10 years ago. The sexual allegation involved Reverend A masturbating his 13-year-old nephew.

> Reverend A acknowledged the sexual interaction with his nephew; however, he emphasized first that this was not "sexual" for him. He gave the following account and went on, in elaborate fashion, to detail how, for some years, the boy had been sexually aggressive with him. For example, he indicated that the boy had asked to shower with him. In addition, he said that the boy had laid his head on his (Reverend A's) lap on several occasions while watching television. During the event in question, Reverend A reported that he was under the influence of alcohol. The nephew and his family were visiting Reverend A. He stated that he did not normally drink, but his brother (the boy's father) had cajoled him into having a couple of drinks. He later learned that his brother had made

"triples." Reverend A went to his room for the night; he was sharing a room with his nephew. The nephew appeared to be feigning sleep and was partially uncovered. Reverend A said he had "had enough" and demanded to know "what's going on?" He asked the boy directly if he was sexually attracted to him, and the boy said he was. He said the boy asked him to touch his genitals, and Reverend A did so. He said that although the boy was aroused, he himself was not. He touched him for a short time, and the boy did not ejaculate. When asked who he felt was responsible for these events, Reverend A stated, "I would hate to say my nephew...he was only 13 at the time." When asked what effects this situation had on the nephew, Reverend A remarked, "I hope nothing; he is married now so I tend to think he is okay."

This case illustrates how Reverend A's defenses actively served to insulate his self-esteem from the full implications of his behavior. Reverend A has construed the events that led to the sexual abuse in a way that casts him as victim, both of his nephew's sexual advances and his brother who gave him too much to drink. For Reverend A, these two are responsible for the situation, and he thereby preserves his sense of being a "good person."

Group therapy is a social interaction where offenders engage in a relationship with other group members and the therapists. This fact is important to remember when considering the relevance of self-esteem in assessing treatment readiness and in gauging apparent progress toward the goals of treatment. Some offenders may be motivated to discuss their offenses, desiring the cathartic effects of discussing the actions that brought stress to their lives and caused harm to others (for an overview of positive consequences of self-disclosure and confession, see Kowalski, 1999). However, because they are unaware of the details of the other group members' offenses, they may believe that their own offenses are the worst ones and that others will view them as "sick":

*Many patients enter therapy with the disquieting thought that
they are unique in their wretchedness, that they alone have
certain frightening or unacceptable problems, thoughts, impulses,
and fantasies (Yalom, as quoted in Kowalski, 1999, p. 231).*

It is important to note that self-esteem is not only conceptualized
as a trait, being relatively stable over time (Rosenberg, 1965), but
it is also believed to vary across situations and fluctuate over time
(Burke, 1980; Campbell & Tesser, 1985; Kernis, 1993; Wells &
Marwell, 1976). Indeed, there is evidence that individuals with
variable, reactive self-esteem are at increased risk to engage in aggressive or violent behavior (see Bushman and Baumeister,
1998). As noted previously, both incarcerated men and
nonincarcerated men who have committed sexual offenses are in
a situation that can have at least temporary, threatening effects on
their self-evaluations. Other offenders condemn sexual offenders, and all sexual offenders face the loss of support from loved
ones. Even for the offenders who had relatively high prior levels
of self-esteem, the circumstances of their present situation can
have a negative impact on their self-evaluations. Therefore, the
points made here are relevant to both offenders who are normally
low in self-esteem as well as those who exhibit high self-esteem
in different environments. And it may be difficult for a therapist
to determine, at least at the outset, which clients have normally
low or high self-esteem. However, sexual offenders with low self-
esteem may be more steadfast in their attempts to avoid risk of
further deprecation during group therapy. People with low self-
esteem perceive themselves to have fewer positive attributes available to reaffirm their integrity when faced with a threat to their
self-esteem (Spencer et al., 1993). Moreover, individuals with low
self-esteem tend not to compensate for threats to their self-image
(Dodgson & Wood, 1998), making them less resilient to threats
than those high in self-esteem. Conversely, those with rigidly
high self-esteem may have the most to lose when considering
their offenses and their role in them (Bushman & Baumeister,

1998). Thus a therapist might expect that clients with fragile or low self-esteem will be more likely to stick to their external attributions, victim blame, and denial of certain aspects of the offense than would clients who are better able to perceive their strengths and thereby sustain a tolerable self-image.

Another potential difficulty with low self-esteem offenders is their tendency to draw attention to the crimes of other offenders in the group in an effort to make themselves appear more favorably. This is akin to downward social comparison (Wills, 1981). The behavior may involve an emphasis on the brutality of another group member's offense to draw attention away from an offender's own crime, thus reducing the threat of negative feedback from group members. These attempts do not always work, however, and must be discouraged to prevent the other group members from retaliating in an effort to protect their own self-images.

Spencer et al. (1993) pointed out that because low self-esteem individuals cannot draw on strengths (because they fail to perceive many strengths in themselves) to buffer against the threat to their self-image, they must use different strategies. Similar to downward social comparison in its generation of negative attention to others, Spencer et al. (1993) indicated that low self-esteem individuals may be more likely than those with high self-esteem to restore their sense of self-worth through displays of prejudice. This process, it is argued, is easier than the process of accessing positive self-evaluation evidence. Therefore, clients with low self-esteem may be more likely to exhibit prejudice when they are in a context that evokes negative self-evaluative thoughts or interpretations. In sexual offender treatment, prejudice can be revealed in the form of statements about groups of people in general. For example, negative statements about women such as "all women are gold-diggers" serve to justify aggressive behavior by attributing provocative or deserving elements to adult female victims. Also, offenders frequently portray police officers and the criminal justice system as "corrupt," while seeing themselves as victims, thereby turning attention away from their crimes and toward another group. In discussions about the criminal justice system, offenders will undoubtedly find allies among other group members, and the focus of the group discussion can quickly digress. For example:

> *During a group discussion of empathy and the effects of sexual abuse on their victims, one group member stated that the police sometimes make it difficult for victims to talk about the offense because they ask them too many questions and are insensitive to the feelings of the victims. He went on to say that the police do not make it any easier for offenders, and "sometimes they even beat you when they're not supposed to." Others in the group quickly joined in, and before long, the discussion had digressed to anecdotes of corrupt police officers, ineffective lawyers, judges who made mistakes, and jury members who should have been screened out during the selection process. The therapist continued writing on the flipchart she had been using to record the effects of sexual abuse on the victims, taking down each point made during the digression. When she asked a vocal group member to read the list of effects on victims back to her, exactly as they appeared on the chart, he realized the turn the discussion had taken. The group continued their discussion but this time with a focus on why they had digressed.*

The above example outlines how offenders attempt to draw sympathy for themselves and divert attention away from the harm they have caused others, which can appear as a lack of empathy. Clearly, such digressions can reflect conscious attempts to shift uncomfortable or critical focus onto others. However, they may also reflect more "automatic" or reflexive self-serving biases aimed at preserving self-esteem (for a review of such biases, see Blaine & Crocker, 1993; Taylor & Brown, 1988). It is important to challenge these tendencies but also, as in the example above, to examine the function that these digressions serve. It can be challenging for a therapist to encourage offenders to consider their thought processes, particularly in clients with elevated hostility levels. Therefore, questions concerning their thinking are optimally posed in a non-confrontational manner, and efforts should be focused on soliciting the responses from clients rather than lecturing them. In fact, lecturing may have a countertherapeutic effect, providing the offender with yet another experience of criticism. When, as in the group example above, offenders discover their own distortions, there is opportunity for therapists to respond supportively. Such responses strengthen the therapeutic alliance and provide an experience of care that hostile individuals tend not to engender in others (for a review of the responses elicited by interpersonal hostility, see Kiesler, 1983). Examining self-serving biases in interpretations and their effects on a client's demonstrations of victim empathy, can promote insight into faults in cognitive processes without focusing on the offenses directly. This exercise can then serve as a step toward examining the biases or distortions in the client's thoughts that contributed directly to the offense cycle.

As a further point to this discussion, Campbell and Lavallee (1993) found that people with low self-esteem show strong affective reactions to feedback from their social environment. Thus, individuals with low self-esteem feel more threatened by negative feedback than do individuals with high self-esteem. We have already noted the implications that this threat of negative feedback carries in the context of treatment, but this research also has implications for the feedback given to clients. Because people with low self-esteem experience stronger affective reactions to negative feedback, they may be more resistant to challenges to their perspectives offered by the therapist. Challenges may be perceived as negative feedback (i.e., the individual interprets such challenges as personal attacks) and may result in the offender displaying counterproductive emotional reactions. Extremely hostile, or otherwise negative emotions in re-action to therapist feedback, are likely due to perceived threats to the client's sense of self-worth. It is important for therapists to keep this in mind, as offenders reacting in this way are less likely, in turn, to engage in adaptive responses.

Thus clients who react strongly to self-relevant feedback might be more inclined to experience negative mood states and marked fluc-tuations in mood. Campbell, Chew, and Scratchley (1991) found that individuals with low self-esteem were more likely than indi-viduals with high self-esteem to experience more fluctuations of mood over a two-week period. In this study, however, judges who rated the nature of the events that triggered the mood fluctuations found no differences in the difficulty or stressfulness of these events. This suggests that differences in reaction to events did not result from the actual differences in the frequency or quality of stressful events. This is important because it suggests that clients who have fluctuating mood states (generally, low self-esteem cli-ents) will not necessarily appraise the process of the group in the same way as those whose moods are less susceptible to such sud-den increases in negative affect (generally, high self-esteem clients).

While people with low self-esteem sometimes employ strategies unlikely to be adaptive in the long run, they are more likely than high self-esteem individuals to avoid such threats in the first place. Clients with low self-esteem may thus be less likely to place themselves in a context where threats to their self-image may be expected. In the context of therapy, an obvious way to avoid the potential threat to self-image is to refuse to participate. In the case of sexual offenders, even though there are several in-centives to participate in treatment programs (e.g., transfer to a lower-security institution or early release for incarcerated offend-ers, avoidance of incarceration for offenders who are on a condi-tional release or who are in the community as an alternative to sentencing), many offenders still do refuse to enroll in group-based treatment programs. Despite the fact that a decision by sexual offenders to refuse to participate in treatment carries negative consequences with it, the process by which the client reaches such a decision can be explained in terms of decisional balance (Janis & Mann, 1977). Thus clients consider both the benefits of participating in treatment along with the costs (i.e., threats to self-image). People with low self-esteem appear more strongly motivated to avoid failure and the consequent negative effect (e.g., Brockner, Derr, & Laing, 1987; Shrauger & Rosenberg, 1970); therefore, they may be more likely than those with high self-esteem to refuse treatment. Unfortunately, these clients will also inevitably have to rationalize their refusal (e.g., to staff members or to loved ones), and they might consequently be tempted to phrase such rationalizations in terms of denial of the offenses or minimization of problems related to the offenses.

Cognitive dissonance theory (Festinger, 1957) has clear application to clients who engaged in offensive behaviors. Cognitive dissonance theory posits feelings of tension result from holding two psychologically inconsistent cognitions (ideas, attitudes, beliefs). Individuals who find themselves in this situation must then attempt to reduce tension by reducing the discrepancy between the cognitions. For example, men who have committed a sexual offense are consequently faced with the formidable task of integrating that behavior within their concept of themselves. In order to do this, they either have to think of their behavior differently to make it more congruent with their self-concept, or they have to alter their self-concept to be more congruent with the behavior. As noted in the previous discussion, efforts to make their behavior a better fit with their self-concept include distorting their presentation of the circumstances of the offenses. Other clients may instead reduce cognitive dissonance by framing their self-concept in a way that is consistent with the offending behavior. Therefore, they may take responsibility for their offenses but conclude that they must be truly "sick" or "evil" people. Clients who adopt this view of themselves demonstrate an inability to separate their views of their offenses from their view of themselves; they may lack the self-concept complexity necessary to integrate both positive and negative aspects of themselves (see Campbell et al., 1991; Campbell, 1990; Linville, 1985, 1987, for reviews of self-complexity). Ideally, treatment should increase complexity of the self-concept, permitting acceptance of responsibility together with confidence to make efforts toward adaptive lifestyle changes. Otherwise, these individuals experience shame, which has been shown to impede change (Tangney & Dearing, 2002). When people are able to distinguish themselves from their behavior (e.g., I am a good person who did a bad thing), they experience guilt about their offensive acts, which has been shown to facilitate beneficial changes (Tangney & Dearing, 2002).

IMPLICATIONS FOR TREATMENT PROGRESS

A self-deprecating response to having offended will negatively impact the offender's ability to progress toward treatment goals. People with low self-esteem already expect to do poorly (Shrauger, 1975), and they believe criticism more than they believe praise (e.g., McFarlin & Blascovich, 1981; Tice, 1993). Individuals with low self-esteem have been found to be less motivated and perform more poorly at tasks after they have been given feedback that indicates failure (Brockner et al., 1987; Baumeister & Tice, 1985). Thus, participants may be less likely, or take longer, to complete homework assignments when there is a heavy evaluative component, creating the anticipation of more negative feedback. For sexual offenders, sharing aspects of themselves relevant to their offenses offers little hope, in their view, of positive feedback or support. Low self-esteem offenders are, therefore, apt to be particularly avoidant of such situations.

The relationship between enhanced self-esteem and motivation to practise tasks (or in this case, complete homework assignments and participate in the group therapy) can be understood in terms of self-efficacy. Bandura (1977) explained self-efficacy as the belief in one's ability to carry out a particular behavior. Self-efficacy can be enhanced by actually engaging in that behavior, observing a model engaging in the behavior successfully, receiving verbal persuasion to carry out the behavior, and feeling calm enough to evaluate one's capabilities with optimism. Therefore, therapists must work with their clients to overcome their fear of failing and set tasks that the client can complete successfully. Beech and Fordham (1997) found that supportive group therapists were more likely to conduct cohesive groups that focused on practical tasks and decision-making. While the supportive therapeutic environment may not be a sufficient condition for producing changes in client behavior, including behavior related to cognitive distortions and empathy deficits, it is clearly necessary.

According to Rodin, Elias, Silberstein, and Wagner (1988), individuals with low self-esteem are less motivated to make commitments to change, but if this is compounded with an ineffective therapeutic relationship, a client may end up feeling worse than if he had never enrolled in treatment in the first place. Such a client may also be quite difficult to engage in future therapeutic endeavors. Considering all of these points, we conclude that it is necessary to provide feedback wherever possible to clients in a manner that enhances their self-esteem so that these clients will be motivated to complete the necessary work to achieve the goals of therapy. Recently, Marshall and his colleagues (Marshall et al., in press) have provided evidence in support of the role of the therapist in facilitating the attainment of treatment goals with sexual offenders, and it is clear that treating clients in such a way as to enhance their sense of self-worth leads to beneficial changes in treatment targets.

Just as the problem behavior (e.g., sexual offending) occurs in the context of predisposing individual factors and precipitating environmental circumstances, behavior change is also affected by similar factors. Therapists must be attuned to the individual differences clients bring with them into therapy. Moreover, therapists must be aware of relevant aspects of clients' environments. As mentioned at the beginning of this chapter, clients receive feedback from a variety of sources outside the context of their therapeutic group. They may have difficulty incorporating negative feedback from outside sources (e.g., media, other offenders, other institutional staff) with the feedback they receive from the therapist and fellow group members. Clients must be given the opportunity to discuss these sources of feedback and their experiences within these contexts if they are to develop a sense of self-efficacy in dealing with these situations in their day-to-day lives.

CONCLUSIONS

In this chapter, we have investigated the presentation of sexual offenders in a group therapy context. We (and other authors in this volume) have reviewed research on empathy that demonstrates equivocal findings in the sexual offender population. We noted the stance of some researchers (Marshall et al., 1995) that apparent empathy deficits are really the manifestation of cognitive distortion. Clearly, there is a need for further research in understanding empathy with this population, including the development of measures sensitive not only to the affective components of empathy but also to the cognitive and behavioral components. Through further examination of the types of cognitive distortions relevant to sexual offenders, we have concluded here and elsewhere (Marshall et al., 1999) that cognitive distortions are methods of defending against the threats to self-worth inherent in taking responsibility for sexual crimes. The overall conclusion one can draw from this review is that when working with

sexual offenders, as with any other population, one must look beyond the symptoms (whether they are empathy deficits, cognitive
distortions, or low self-esteem) in order to efficiently target interventions and achieve the goals of treatment. Readers interested
in further material relating to empathy, cognitive distortions, and
self-esteem in sexual offenders may refer to Fernandez, Anderson, and Marshall (1999).

6

EMOTIONAL EXPRESSION & RECOGNITION

G. Serran

"The energy that actually shapes the world springs from emotions."
George Orwell (1903-1950)

As mentioned in the first chapter of this book, the term empathy has generated a plethora of definitions, most of which have at least some aspects in common. Recent conceptualizations of empathy have included both cognitive processes (e.g., recognition of another person's emotional states and ability to take another's perspective), and emotional responsiveness (e.g., feeling another's feelings). Underlying the cognitive process and, to some degree, the emotional response of empathy is the ability to accurately identify and label emotions, either in ourselves or in others. In fact, Marshall, Hudson, Jones, and Fernandez's (1995) multi-stage model of empathy notes that the unfolding of the empathic process is dependent upon the preceding stages, the first of which is recognition of another person's emotional state. In addition, we will see later in the Chapter on Empathy Training the vast majority of empathy enhancement strategies include a component on identifying emotions in others. Given that the ability or lack of ability to appropriately recognize emotions in others appears to be so integral to empathy that we felt a review of the literature on that specific component of empathy would be necessary.

Emotions

Emotional experience and expression comprise the thoughts, feelings, and behaviors that combine to create our interpersonal interactions. Emotions are complex, patterned reactions to events that involve various components and influence social interactions, and when an emotion is maintained over a period of time, it is considered a "mood." Emotions are described as internal affective states, rather than bodily, cognitive, or behavioral states (Ortony, Clore, & Foss, 1987). They may be triggered by external events (e.g., by something someone else says or does or by good or bad news), or they may be initiated internally (e.g., by negatively reflecting on current circumstances). Clore, Schwartz, and Conway (1994) point out that rejection, for example, results from the action of another person while the internal states, resulting from the perception of being rejected (e.g., sadness, anger), are emotions. Similarly, bodily states such as pain, cognitive states such as confusion, and behavioral states such as aggressiveness are not considered emotional states. Ekman and Friesen (1975) claim there are about six "primary" emotions (anger, sadness, happiness, surprise, fear, and disgust), which people are biologically primed to experience and recognize. The authors state that other emotions are learned and are usually a combination of these basic emotions.

Emotions serve a number of functions, including communicating to and influencing others. Both verbal and nonverbal forms of emotional expression allow for different ways of delivering messages to others. Charles Darwin (1872), for example, suggested that the facial expression of emotions was the primary means by which all mammals (including humans) convey their emotional states to both conspecifics and members of other species. In addition, emotions can organize and motivate our own behavior. For example, guilt prevents harmful behavior, test anxiety promotes studying, and determination promotes action. In this way, emotions provide us with information about our circumstances. If we learn to trust and recognize emotions, they can serve as positive or negative signs that may contribute to decision-making. From an evolutionary perspective, emotions permit us to adapt to our environment (Izard, 1992). For example, emotions help humans and other primates minimize rejection, avoid attack, and achieve cooperation (Miller & Leary, 1992).

INTERPERSONAL COMMUNICATION OF EMOTION

The primary function of emotion is to communicate needs and feelings to others, and most emotional experience occurs within interpersonal interaction. Social interaction produces a wide range of emotions such as joy, love and affection, anger, fear, sadness, guilt or shame, and jealousy. For example, an individual might become angry in response to another person's insults, criticism, incompetent behavior (e.g., thoughtlessness) or relationship-threatening behavior (e.g., unfaithfulness). Anger is one of the most powerful emotions, and its overt expressions function to communicate the person's motivation and potentially dangerous state to others. Anger is typically shown through making an angry facial expression, having a severe tone of voice, breaking things, slamming doors, making threatening gestures, or staring in a hostile way (Guerrero, 1994; Shaver, Krison, & O'Connor, 1987). Anger is also expressed verbally through making nasty or sarcastic comments, interrupting, blaming, and challenging. Some individuals, however, may deny feeling angry, which typically allows anger to build until it is no longer tolerable. Both guilt and shame occur when individuals feel they have committed some negative act against others. Guilt, however, is often focused on a specific behavior while shame pertains to an overall negative view of self. Interestingly, guilt often involves direct communication designed to repair the situation while shame usually results in avoidance. Happiness is one of the most common positive emotions and is usually communicated through positive facial displays (e.g., smiling, laughing, talking enthusiastically) (Ekman, Friesen, & Ellsworth, 1972). Love is expressed through patterns of disclosure, hugging and kissing, smiling, and other forms of affection. Sadness is generally communicated to others through gloomy facial expressions, crying, reduced smiling, moping, or speaking in a monotone voice (Ekman et al., 1972). Sad individuals often have more difficulty focusing on others during conversation. Research suggests that social support seeking, sharing problems, increasing activity level, and thinking about positive experiences or about positive aspects to life are healthy responses to sadness, whereas social withdrawal and dwelling on miserable thoughts are likely to keep the individual feeling sad (Nolen-Hoeksema, 1987). Each of these emotions are social emotions and serve to communicate to others.

People bring all of these emotional states into their interactions with others, and these emotions significantly influence how they behave toward others. People who are happy usually respond with warmth toward others, whereas those who are in negative moods may behave in a hostile or withdrawn manner. People's emotions can also change through social interaction. Thus, people's goals, expectations, and emotional understanding influence their responses to others as well as their ability to understand and express their own emotions.

RECOGNITION AND EXPRESSION OF EMOTIONS

Most people express their own or recognize others' emotions by using facial cues such as smiles, frowns, eye-contact, gritting teeth, etc. (Scherer, Wallbott, Matsumoto, & Kudoh, 1988). Researchers have found that people are quite accurate at recognizing a limited set of emotions through facial expressions even across cultures, with some emotions being more difficult to recognize than others. For example, negative emotions are more easily confused with one another than are positive emotions, and simple emotions are easier to identify than emotional blends (Ekman, 1993; Ekman & O'Sullivan, 1991). Research has suggested that specific client populations often seem to lack empathy (e.g., offenders) and demonstrate deficiencies in their ability to identify emotions (McCown, Johnson, & Austin, 1986; Hudson et al., 1993). Chronically delinquent male adolescents have been found less accurate in identifying the facial expressions of sadness, surprise, and disgust compared to a similar sample of nondelinquents (McCown et al., 1986). Similarly, Hudson et al. (1993) determined that sexual offenders were less accurate than violent offenders and nonoffender groups at identifying emotions in both adults and children. The emotions these sexual offenders had difficulty with were anger, fear, and disgust, each of which they typically confused with surprise. Certainly, some inaccuracies are more problematic than others. In most social situations, confusing emotions that are subtly different is not likely to be a major concern, but gross inadequacies in accurately perceiving other's emotions may become more problematic, particularly if it leads to inappropriate or even harmful behaviors.

Although vocal cues are less frequently researched than facial cues, they still provide important clues as to an individual's emotions (e.g., Frick, 1985). For example, screaming, yelling, speaking with a shaky voice, or using pressured speech are all expressions of emotion. Verbal cues, (e.g., choice of words) also provide emotional information. For example, when we are angry, we may curse, verbally attack, and complain; when we are sad we may criticize ourselves; and when we are happy we may say positive things (Shaver et al., 1987). Finally, body language is yet another form of emotional expression. Gait characteristics such as arm swing, length of stride, walking slowly or walking quickly can all assist in distinguishing sadness from happiness or anger (Walters & Walk, 1988). Additionally, actions such as hugging, kissing, engaging in sexual activity, hitting, walking away, leaning toward, and physical proximity all provide some indication of warmth in interpersonal relationships (Shaver et al., 1987). In most social interaction, a variety of cues are used for interpretation of emotional expression. From a therapeutic standpoint the diversity offers ample opportunity to gain additional insight into clients affective states by assessing inconsistent cues (e.g., conflicting verbal expression and body language).

EXPRESSION VERSUS NON-EXPRESSION

Effective emotional expression involves the ability to convey a message in a manner that produces a desired effect. This likely includes clearly communicating feelings while taking into account the perspective of others as well as the relevant social norms.

How important is it to express what we feel? The consequences of emotional expression may be either positive or negative, depending on what and how it is expressed. For example, expressing anger through physical aggression or by yelling may have serious consequences; on the other hand, "holding in" anger may also have many negative consequences. Numerous studies have demonstrated mental and physical health benefits associated with emotional expression and psychophysiological costs associated with inhibited expression (Pennebaker, 1995). Thus, flexibility and some ability to weigh the pros and cons of emotional expression are important skills. Clinical interventions should aim to help clients achieve such a balance in their emotional behavior.

PARENTAL MODELING, DIRECTIVES, & EXPECTANCIES

Emotion is particularly important in social interactions. Individuals must correctly read and respond to the emotions of others as well as modulate their own emotional behavior for successful social relationships. Research on emotional socialization has examined these abilities in children (e.g., Eisenberg & Fabes, 1992; Fox, 1995). A number of viewpoints have been presented, but the way in which parents respond to emotional distress is believed to have implications for the child's cognitive and social development. For example, Malatesta and Haviland (1982) stated that differences exist in the way mothers respond to the facial expressions of infants, depending on the infant's gender. Research on sex differences suggests that women may develop a greater repertoire of emotional expression because parents display a greater range of emotions when interacting with girls (Brody & Hall, 1993).

"Display rules" of what is "okay" to express and what is "not okay" to express are learned during childhood. Parental directives such as "boys don't cry," "calm down," and "everything is okay," teach children what emotions are not acceptable. Negative emotions are often punished, particularly for girls, and angry children are often sent to their rooms and made to feel guilty (Stearns, 1989). These experiences affect the way children respond and learn about emotions, which in turn affects interpersonal communication and response to others. Clinical interventions can help clients reconsider their early socialization and belief patterns in terms of current circumstances.

EMOTIONAL INSIGHT/RECOGNITION

Possessing insight into emotion involves the ability to recognize, accurately label, and understand both one's own emotional experience and that of others. Emotional recognition and understanding provides individuals with information about themselves and their environment (Schwarz, 1990). Most therapeutic interventions typically seek to help clients understand and interpret their emotional experience and the expression of emotions by others

(Kennedy-Moore, 1999) based on the belief that if clients understand their own feelings and the causes of those feelings, then they will be better equipped to cope adaptively. Those lacking in emotional understanding frequently display little insight, respond to issues in a concrete manner, and frequently do not understand their decisions, as in the following example.

> *Morris was participating in a group for men who had sexually offended. Throughout Morris' life, he had faced numerous traumatic experiences, specifically emotional abuse from his mother and physical abuse from his father. As he developed, Morris began shutting others out and had numerous failed relationships. However, when asked about these experiences, Morris minimized the effect of his childhood experiences, blamed his partners for the problems in their relationships, and he did not appear overly upset about the difficulties in his life. He presented as relatively flat and struggled to describe any of his emotions. "Life goes on," said Morris, shrugging his shoulders after being asked how he felt about his most recent relationship problems.*

In order to regulate negative affect (Kennedy-Moore, 1999) and to develop a sense of self (Watson & Greenberg, 1996), individuals need to be able to recognize and understand their emotions. Extremely upsetting events such as childhood trauma and broken relationships often elicit numerous emotions such as anger, betrayal, abandonment, loneliness, and guilt. As in Morris' case, inability to recognize these emotions carries over into interpersonal relationships and makes it impossible to respond to the other person's emotions. Morris learned as a child that being vulnerable was frightening. Therefore, emotions that make him feel vulnerable, such as fear or love, become terrifying, and he quickly learned to hide such displays of emotion. However, as an adult, this strategy had negative consequences, particularly by limiting his ability to function effectively and communicate in intimate relationships (Buck, 1989).

As noted earlier, the events that prompt or elicit emotions may be internal or external to the individual. A person's own thoughts, behaviors, and physical reactions may prompt emotions, and one emotion may prompt another. Most events, however, do not automatically result in emotions. Emotions occur as a result of the person's interpretation of the event. Emotions involve changes in central nervous system activity with some specific areas of the brain (e.g., the limbic system) appearing very important. Emotions also involve alterations in other bodily functions such as muscle activity and blood pressure, fluctuations in heart rate, and changes in skin temperature. Among these various changes in muscle activity are alterations in facial expressions that correspond to various emotional states. As noted earlier, Darwin (1872) saw these facial expressions of emotion as critical to emotional recognition, and he believed these cues provided information vital to survival. In the course of evolutionary history, Darwin said, the individuals incapable of correctly identifying emotions in others (e.g., the anger involved in threat displays) were unlikely to survive and pass on their genetic endowment. Ekman and his colleagues (see Ekman & Friesen, 1975, for a summary of their research) have pursued this line of research with humans for the past several decades, and their findings have markedly increased our understanding of the bases of emotional recognition.

Labeling and identifying our current emotions can be difficult because emotions are complex behavioral responses (Linehan, 1988). Effective identification involves not only the ability to accurately observe our internal responses but to also describe the context in which these responses are generated. Thus, identification of an emotional response is assisted through 1) the ability to describe the event eliciting the particular emotion; 2) the interpretation of the event that prompts a particular emotion (e.g., what thoughts are experienced?); 3) the bodily sensations (e.g., racing heart, "seeing red," a lump in the throat, etc.); 4) the behaviors expressing the emotion; and 5) the aftereffects of the emotion on particular aspects of functioning.

Kennedy-Moore and Watson (1999) identify five aspects of emotional awareness:

1. Physiological sensations such as "I feel tired" or "I feel tightness in my gut"
2. Bodily action tendencies: "I feel like hitting someone"
3. Single differentiated emotion: "I feel happy"
4. Combinations of differentiated emotions: "I feel angry and sad"
5. Differentiated feelings of self and other: "I'm disappointed that I didn't get an A on my paper, but I'm happy that my friend did."

At lower levels of emotional functioning, individuals have minimal recognition of their emotions while at the higher levels, they have a complex, elaborated understanding of the quality and intensity of their feelings. It is also important to be aware that some people who show significant insight regarding some emotional topics may show minimal recognition in other areas. This is particularly true for circumstances that, for example, generate both threats and compassion. For example, family caregivers of a patient with Alzheimer's disease may be aware of their sadness and feelings of loss but are less able to acknowledge their feelings of anger and resentment about having to care for their loved one.

The abilities to express or communicate emotions are important elements in recognizing emotions, and they are thought to be critical during the decoding stage of social processing (McFall, 1982) and in the ability to respond empathically to distress in others (Marshall, Jones, Hudson, & McDonald, 1993). As mentioned previously, emotions are communicated verbally and nonverbally (e.g., facial expressions). Ekman, Levenson, and Friesen (1983) suggest that the expression of primary emotions is "hard-wired" in humans in the sense that the same facial expressions are innately linked to the same basic emotions. However, people often learn to inhibit emotional expressions or to express them differently. For more complex emotions, the ability to express these must be learned and are thus influenced by cultural factors. Different facial expressions and behaviors may express different emotions, depending on the person's culture, family patterns, and peer relationships as well as arising from individual differences. Therapeutically, this point may be vitally important as individuals from cultures other than our own (e.g., Aboriginals), may be less emotionally expressive or express emotions in a manner not immediately apparent to the therapist.

For therapists, it may be difficult at times to determine whether a client is not experiencing negative feelings or whether they lack insight into their emotions. This distinction may be critical as those who are "tuned out" to what they are feeling are often unable to utilize effective coping strategies. Some of the following techniques have been suggested, Lewis & Haviland-Jones (2000), Kennedy-Moore (1999), Waldron (1996), Safran & Segal (1990), as useful in determining whether or not a client has difficulty recognizing emotions:

1) Emotional memories: The therapist inquires about memories of situations that evoked specific emotions. For example, the therapist could ask a client to describe a situation from memory that caused him or her to feel anger. A client who claims to never have felt anger clearly lacks insight.

2) Situational context: The therapist inquires about certain life situations (e.g., death of a loved one) that typically elicit particular emotions (e.g., feelings of grief).

Therapists should keep in mind, however, that individuals might respond differently to such traumatic events.

3) Identifying signs of emotional blocking: The therapist may look for indicators of "blocking" when the client is discussing feelings (e.g., "I'm feeling something, but I'm not certain how to describe it.").

4) Covert indicators: The therapist may monitor the client's nonverbal behaviors. A client may claim he is not angry when his face is red, he is clenching his fists, and his tone of voice has changed. Once the therapist has determined that the client is indeed lacking insight, then therapy may be focused on improving the client's ability to label and identify emotions before moving toward improving coping strategies.

Effect on Empathy

As mentioned previously, Marshall et al. (1995) construed empathy as a four-stage process involving the ability to recognize another's emotional state, to see the world as the other person does, to experience the same or similar emotional state as the other person, and to make an appropriate response. According to this view, the ability to be "empathic" is dependent upon the ability to recognize emotions and express affect appropriately. In many cases, it is necessary for clients to develop recognition skills and the ability to express their emotions particularly for more successful relationships and for effective coping, and to serve as a signal that they are living a healthy or unhealthy lifestyle. Being emotionally expressive is also an important characteristic for therapists to display. Research has shown that therapists' displays of empathy and warmth, for example, facilitate treatment changes in various clients (Marshall et al., in press) as well as in sexual offenders (Serran, Fernandez, Marshall, & Mann, in press).

In various situations, clients may have difficulty experiencing and expressing emotions, which is likely to have numerous negative consequences. For example, the inability to acknowledge and express emotions may contribute to substance abuse with the intent of "dulling" emotions, it may result in lack of insight and responsibility for behavior, or it may produce insensitivity and aggressive behavior. In our society, people are frequently given the message that they should smile even when unhappy, be nice and "not rock the boat" when angry. Similarly, we often quickly try to reduce unpleasant emotions even when it may be appropriate to feel badly. For clinicians, all of these issues present important treatment considerations. Therapists should attempt to understand their clients' abilities to recognize their own emotions and those of other people, their understanding of the various emotions, and their choice of emotional expression. Then therapists should help clients develop a balance of emotional repertoire in order to facilitate effective interpersonal relationships.

TREATMENT IMPLICATIONS

Techniques for Emotional Recognition

Carich, Henderson-Odum, and Metzger, (2001) identified a number of strategies that may be used to help clients develop emotional recognition. They suggest that clients define and differentiate between thoughts and feelings; keep a journal highlighting clients' reactions to events; learn basic feelings such as anger, sadness, happiness, distress, apathy, anxiety, and confusion; write an autobiography and identify feelings in response to various events in their lives; focus on discussing immediate experiences. This approach may be particularly effective during therapy when the therapist notices a particular reaction in a client.

Clients may be asked to describe events from their past that they remember as particularly distressing (see Marshall, Anderson, & Fernandez, 1999). They can then be encouraged to relive the experience and express their feelings as accurately as possible. This technique is particularly effective for clients who have "built walls" around themselves and refuse to experience vulnerable emotions. For example, the client may be asked to recall the loss of a loved one, the ending of an intimate relationship, or physical, emotional, or sexual abuse as a child. In group therapy, other participants can be asked to identify their own feelings after hearing another individual's experience.

Some clients lack the skills to interpret and label their feelings. It may also help to have the client develop symbolization through labeling his inner states and helping the client interpret his emotions by looking at how his feelings are related to his goals, values, needs, and desires. Among specific techniques is "empathic reflection," which involves statements by the therapist that attempt to uncover buried thoughts and feelings. "Evocative empathy responses" (Rice, 1974), which involve the use of colorful, imagistic language can help bring a client's experiences to life. Similarly, "systematic evocative unfolding" (Rice & Saperia, 1984) is useful when clients report being puzzled by their emotional reactions. In this case, having clients vividly describe a scene and assisting them in identifying the triggers to their reactions can be helpful.

"Motivated lack of awareness" of emotions is a more difficult issue to address clinically. In this situation, clients suppress conscious awareness of their feelings due to the threat involved. Thus, a strong therapeutic alliance is critically important. Clients need to feel safe in order to stop hiding from their threatening feelings. Helpful techniques in this case involve assisting the client in recognizing signs of emotional blocking (e.g., the client might divert to another topic, "freeze" when discussing certain topics, or engage in "chatty," rapid speech). Therapists should remember to be gentle, inquire about what is happening for the client at the moment, and not push the client. Instead, the therapist should explore the block and prompt the client to examine what is going on emotionally. Another technique involves drawing attention to the client's nonverbals signs of emotion. Therapists can comment on their client's facial or bodily expression (e.g., scowling, clenching fists, closed body language). The client may say he feels fine but appear listless or unhappy. In these cases, the therapist should point out, "you're saying you feel okay, but you look sad."

Techniques for Encouraging Emotional Expression

In order to effectively express emotions, it is necessary for the client to first recognize how he is feeling. Once he is able to distinguish between various feeling states (e.g., anger versus hurt), he will be in a better position to express feelings. Asking questions can help encourage emotional expression, and in some cases, direct identification of a feeling state may be necessary. Some clients may not be aware of their emotions in which case the therapist may express his/her opinion of what emotion might be a typical response to the situation described. Clients may reflect back on previous experiences and express how they felt at that time. Asking open-ended questions is a useful approach to help clients develop a more in-depth understanding of their feelings. For example, the therapist might ask, "What would it mean to you if you allowed yourself to express your feelings?" "What do you fear might happen?" Or "How likely is it that the worst possible case might happen?" This process helps clients recognize irrational beliefs and examine the more probable consequences.

The therapist should keep in mind that some clients may feel inhibited from expressing emotions due to negative messages regarding emotional expression that were learned in childhood. As mentioned earlier, they may have learned at a young age that particular emotions (e.g., anger, sadness) are not acceptable or that expressing emotions is inappropriate or immasculine. Additionally, they may not have had appropriate models who demonstrated regular expressions of emotion. Thus, identifying the particular life experiences of the client may be important in addition to creating a new experience for the client. Similarly, clients may even be afraid or anxious at the idea of expressing particular emotions. For example, some clients indicate that they are afraid that if they begin crying, they will never stop. In this situation, helping clients recognize the goals and value of certain emotions provides them with the opportunity to reexamine and revise their beliefs.

Cognitive restructuring may be used to get past emotional "blocks" or defenses that clients use to protect themselves. This can be achieved by identifying what might be inhibiting emotional expression, challenging the clients' view, and helping them see things from a different perspective. For example, a discussion may center around the belief that sadness is not an acceptable emotion for men and that crying is not allowed. This belief may be challenged to develop a healthier viewpoint. Similarly, anger is frequently not an acceptable emotional response for women. As a result, women may turn their anger 'inward' and experience it as depression or anxiety. In these cases, validating the clients' experience and assisting her in expressing anger in a healthy way may be a useful strategy.

A variety of other techniques have been used to enhance emotional expression. For example, role-plays have been used to help express emotions more effectively (See Chapter 8 on using role play to enhance empathy), and relaxation techniques or meditation may assist in helping clients feel less defensive and more willing to express various emotions.

"Flooded expression" occurs when clients show intense levels of emotional arousal, and their feelings seem to be "out of control." They may describe this as "not thinking clearly" and struggle to organize their thoughts or to consider other viewpoints. Their behavior may be impulsive and extreme. In this case, clients need to learn to acknowledge responsibility for their own feelings and talk about feelings in the context of a specific instance rather than generalizing to all instances. The primary therapeutic task in this case is to help clients contain their feelings sufficiently to address the problem. That is, the therapist should work to help the client achieve some distance from their emotions so they can examine their feelings without being completely overwhelmed (Scheff, 1979). One experiential technique used to do this involves "grounding," or focusing on the concrete details of the situation (Briere, 1989; McCann & Pearlman, 1990). Arousal regulation skills such as relaxation techniques, self-talk strategies, and self-soothing are all helpful techniques for these purposes. Teaching active listening skills to help the client concentrate on what the other person is saying can also make the client feel more in control of his emotions. Clients may also benefit from communication skills training to help them express their feelings in assertive rather than aggressive ways.

In cases where ambiguous emotional expression is a problem (e.g., giving expressions that are too subtle, mixed signals, or an unintended expression), the client may not be able to convey the desired emotional message. This problem usually results from anxiety and poor social skills. Therapists should help clients understand their feelings more clearly and provide them with direct feedback concerning how their behavior is perceived by others. Practicing different styles and strategies of communication through role-plays can assist in clearing up ambiguity. Additionally, social skills training may be helpful. In sharp contrast, overly responsive emotional arousal may also be problematic. For example, if we look at the concept of "distress proneness," it appears (Costa & McCrae, 1988; Eysenck & Eysenck, 1985; Zuckerman, 1995) that those labeled as high in negative affectivity feel a wide variety of negative emotions on a frequent basis. These individuals tend to focus on negative aspects of their experiences and express a great deal of distress. Interpersonally, they behave in demanding and hostile ways and experience greater social conflict than others (Clark & Watson, 1991). Therapeutically, the relevant focus for these people is to address their propensity to feel distressed in the first place. Similarly, frequent and intense expressions of anger tend to increase rather than decrease angry feelings. Different forms of anger expression have different consequences. For example, very intense anger expression increases arousal while moderated anger expression (e.g., calm discussion) produces milder arousal. Some strategies to achieve a calmer approach include teaching clients to take a "time out" prior to or count to 10 prior to addressing the issue. Clients should come to an understanding that anger expression is most useful when it is directed at the appropriate target, does not lead to further retaliation, and results in beneficial changes.

CONCLUSIONS

Clearly, this chapter highlights how awareness of our emotional states is important in empathy development and healthy functioning. However, simply recognizing how we are feeling is not enough. After acknowledging how we feel, we then need to make decisions about whether we want to express particular emotions. Although therapists often believe that expression of emotion by their clients is essential to effective therapy, there may be times when such expressions are not appropriate or occasions where the goal is to cope with a client's "overexpression." Emotional expression can result in enhanced self-understanding and greater self-acceptance (Mergenthaler, 1996); however, expression that is prolonged or extremely intense can elicit interpersonal rejection.

In cases of expressing sad emotions or discussing traumatic experiences, inhibiting distress may be detrimental. Additionally, simply expressing the emotions will not help if the individual is not able to make some sense of his or her emotions. Therefore, therapists need to determine where the problem lies (lack of recognition, lack of expression–motivated or not, or excessive expression) and assist clients to find a balance between logic and emotion (Greenberg, Rice, & Elliot, 1993). The techniques identified in this chapter may be used as a guide for therapists working with clients who struggle with emotional awareness or expression.

7

Empathy Training for Therapists & Clients

Y. M. Fernandez & G. Serran

"The art of teaching is the art of assisting discovery."
Mark Van Doren (1894-1972)

Despite the lack of consensus regarding the definition of empathy, theoreticians appear to agree that empathy is an important skill for all humans. In fact, it has been described as "perhaps one of the most basic and necessary skills in human communication" (Barak, Engle, Katzir, & Fisher, 1988, p. 458). Thus far in this book, we have focused primarily on the importance of empathy for potential clients. We noted in Chapter 6 on Emotional Expression and Recognition that poor empathy skills may contribute to difficult social interactions or poor intimacy levels in relationships. In addition, previous chapters have described how social intelligence plus a lack of empathy may contribute to aggressive behavior and that empathy deficits are often manifested as cognitive distortions in sexual offenders with low self-esteem. Given that empathic skills appear to be quite central to human interactions, it is not surprising that empathy is considered crucial to therapeutic interactions. We will begin this chapter by briefly reviewing the literature related to empathy in therapists. We will then describe the various popular approaches to training therapists to be more empathic. Finally, we will end the chapter by reviewing strategies for training empathy in clients.

Therapist Empathy

In the clinical literature, the conceptualization of empathy as an important therapist feature has mainly arisen within humanistic and psychoanalytic frameworks. Rogers (1957) described empathy as one of the necessary and sufficient conditions therapists must display to generate client change. Rogers claimed accurate, empathic understanding was "to sense the client's private world as if it were your own, but without ever losing the 'as if' quality– this is empathy, and this seems essential to therapy" (p. 99). Truax and Carkhuff (1967) define empathy as "the skill with which the therapist is able to know and communicate the client's inner being" (p. 5). This definition clearly emphasizes the cognitive processes involved in empathy. Psychoanalytic theorists, on the other hand, tend to emphasize the therapist's affective understanding. In this view, empathy is "the inner experience of sharing and comprehending the momentary psychological state of another person" (Shafer, 1967; p. 343).

Regardless of the conceptual approach, empathy is viewed as integral to establishing and facilitating a good working relationship between client and therapist (Gladstein, 1983). While empathy is not the only characteristic therapists need to display in order to work effectively with clients, it appears to be one of the necessary characteristics. In fact, psychologists frequently assume a causal relationship between empathy and altruism such that empathy motivates helping. Thus, empathy may not only be necessary for understanding the client but also for motivating a desire to help the client.

Research Findings

Empathy is the most extensively researched therapist characteristic with overall findings suggesting that it is a critical feature displayed by effective therapists. The majority of this research has been conducted within therapeutic orientations such as humanistic psychology (Rogers, 1957) or psychoanalytic therapy (Kohut, 1990), but empathy has always been widely recognized as important by therapists within a cognitive behavioral orientation as well (Keijsers, Schapp, & Hoogduin, 2000). For example, a positive correlation has been observed between therapist empathy and problem-solving in delinquent children (Kendall & Wilcox, 1980) such that therapist empathy had the effect of increasing self-control at the end of treatment as well as at follow-up assessment.

Confrontational styles have classically been popular among treatment programs aimed at substance abusers (Miller & Rollnick, 1991) and 'difficult' clients such as sexual offenders or domestic abusers (Marshall, Anderson, & Fernandez, 1999). However, confrontational styles, which tend to have aggressive elements, negate the use of empathy, and research suggests that such a style may be damaging (Annis & Chan, 1983; Beech & Fordham, 1997; Patterson & Forgatch, 1985), In contrast, more positive therapeutic outcomes have been associated with a style emphasizing what Rogers termed "accurate empathy." For example, Miller, Benefield, and Tonigan (1993) compared client-centered counseling with directive-confrontational counseling and found that confrontation was predictive of more client drinking at the one-year follow-up. Miller and Sovereign (1989) randomly assigned half of their substance abusers to a confrontational therapist and the remainder to a challenging but supportive therapist. Clients in the supportive group participated more effectively in therapy and showed significant reductions in alcohol use at follow-up. In yet another study (Miller, Taylor, & West, 1980), different types of treatments for problem-drinking were examined, and independent raters ranked the degree to which therapists displayed empathy. The degree of accurate empathy was a strong predictor of client outcome (abstinence or controlled drinking) and accounted for 67% of the variance in the effectiveness of the therapists.

In a recent study examining treatment-related changes among sexual offenders (Marshall et al., in press), empathy was found (along with warmth, directiveness, and rewarding behavior) to have the greatest impact on client change following treatment.

What Makes an Empathic Therapist?

An empathic therapist tries to see things from the client's point of view and attempts to share the client's world. Empathic therapists have been described as being able to communicate to the client that they take the relationship seriously, both in their tone of voice and their behavior (making eye contact, leaning forward, using "open" body language, nodding, reflecting what the client says, using a warm, friendly tone, modifying voice appropriately); demonstrate they are aware of how the client is feeling at the moment; show they are sensitive and aware of how they feel about the client and how the client is feeling toward them; and communicate the belief that the client can change (e.g., by focusing on future goals, highlighting changes, encouraging the client).

Bachelor (1988) has suggested that there are four different types of therapist empathy, all of which assist the client in different ways. The first type of empathy he calls Cognitive (Facilitative) empathy, which is a reformulation or interpretation by the therapist that helps the client gain a different perspective. In this type, the therapist is empathic when accurately recognizing the client's ongoing inner experience, state, or motivation. A second aspect of Bachelor's definition of cognitive empathy concerns its therapeutic effect such that it will increase self-disclosure, self-understanding, or a positive personality change. The therapist may, for example, reflect back to the client what he or she has said, in order to demonstrate understanding. The therapist "mirrors" what the client is saying in a non-judgemental way, grasping the "essence" of what the client is feeling.

The second type of empathy according to Bachelor is called Affective empathy, which communicates understanding and provides comfort. The client experiences this type of empathy as the therapist participating in the client's emotional state at that moment. The therapist acknowledges the client's feelings and asks an open-ended question to see if he or she is reading the client correctly. For example, the therapist may respond with "It sounds like..." or "What you seem to be saying is...," followed by an expression of what the therapist guesses the client may be feeling. This process helps bring the client's feelings to the forefront. If a client is angrily focusing on the behavior of his or her spouse, the therapist may point out the feelings of hurt or betrayal underlying this anger.

Sharing empathy is the third type described by Bachelor and involves communicating to the client that he or she is not alone and that there are solutions to the problems. The therapist may self-disclose either relevant personal experiences or how s/he is feeling at that moment. This type of empathy generally involves the use of "I feel" statements, followed by an expression of how the therapist is feeling. This is important, as frequently the therapist's feelings reflect what is occurring in the session.

Finally, Bachelor's fourth type of empathy, "Nurturant empathy," provides the client with emotional support and a feeling of security. Clients describe this type of empathy as a sense of an attentive presence, the caring, protective nature of the therapist. Carkhuff and Pierce (1975) suggest that the ability of therapists to demonstrate empathy may reflect different levels of sophistication. They defined five different levels. Level 1 refers to a lack of empathy. The therapist's response either detracts from the client's feelings or fails to recognize what the client is experiencing. Typically, a therapist at this level will give reassurance or advice as opposed to responding to what the client is saying. At Level 2, the response focuses only on the content of what the client says but ignores the feelings of the client (e.g., "So, you think your partner is angry with you?"). Level 3 involves repeating the feelings of the client without adding any new formulations (Client: "I feel really alone right now." Therapist: "You're telling me you feel lonely."). At Level 4 the therapist adds something new to her response to the client's emotions but has difficulty helping the client discover a solution to the problem. (Client: "I just don't know how I'm going to survive without him." Therapist: "What strikes me right now is the hopelessness and uncertainty you are expressing."). Finally, at Level 5, the therapist displays sensitivity to the client's feelings and adds an action step to help the client solve the problem. (Client: "I just don't know how I'm going to survive without him." Therapist: "What strikes me right now is the hopelessness and uncertainty you are expressing. I am also struck by the fact that you have gotten by so far; what have you been doing up until now? Let's explore this in more detail."). Carkhuff and Pierce claim that for therapy to be minimally effective the therapist must display empathy at least at Level 3.

Interestingly, current conceptualizations of empathy have primarily focused on the therapist's empathic attitude and communication, rarely considering the client's experience and perception of the therapist. However, Bachelor's (1988) research suggests that client's perceive the same display of empathy differently. Thus, if the therapist relies on one standard style of empathic response such as reformulating the client's communication then he or she may not be successful with all clients. Barrett-Lennard (1981) presented a model to describe the total empathic interaction between therapist and client, which consists of five sequential steps. The first two steps involve the therapist's attention to the client's feelings, step 3 involves the therapist communicating empathy to the client, and steps 4 and 5 involve client perception and feedback. While Barrett-Lennard identified similar styles of empathy as Bachelor (1988), he emphasizes the importance of the clients perception of the therapist's response. As a result, it is suggested that future research in this area focus more on the client's perception, particularly since it is this that seems to determine treatment outcome. If the client feels understood, then the relationship between the client and therapist is enhanced, and the client may be more willing to make themselves vulnerable within the context of therapy.

Training Therapists to Be Empathic

The obvious question that arises from the conclusion that empathy is necessary for those in the "helping professions" is "To what extent can we teach therapists to be more empathic?" Fortunately, the evidence on counselor training suggests it is possible to effectively teach empathy in addition to other therapeutic skills to both professionals and paraprofessionals. Although a number of empathy training packages described in the literature have little, if any, evidence to support them (e.g., Lewis, 1988), some of the more systematic approaches to therapeutic training have generated sufficient research to support their efficacy (e.g., Egan, 1975; Ivey, 1971; Truax & Carkhuff, 1967). We will describe these methods in more detail throughout this chapter. Readers should note, however, that these more structured counselor training packages are used to train therapists in a variety of important therapeutic skills, of which one is empathy. For our purposes, however, we will focus on research that has evaluated the ability of these methods to increase therapist empathy.

As noted previously, Roger's (1957) claim that empathic accuracy, genuineness, and warmth are necessary and sufficient therapeutic skills initiated a trend toward more structured and clearly delineated approaches to assessing and teaching counselor skills. Prior to Rogers' series of papers counselor training was often unstructured and ill-defined, relying on individual supervision and on personal psychotherapy or psychoanalysis (Lewis, 1988). Baker and Daniels (1989) describe the "evolution" of counselor training as moving from Rogers' graded experiences toward a more didactic-experiential approach as popularized by Carkhuff and colleagues (Carkhuff, 1969; Truax and Carkhuff, 1967). Counselor training was then further systematized by Ivey who introduced "microcounseling," a systematic method for teaching counseling skills in a short period of time (Ivey, 1971).

Rogers' graded experiences required students to listen to tape-recorded interviews, observe live interviews by their supervisor, participate in group and personal therapy, conduct individual psychotherapy, and record their own interviews for discussion with their supervisor (Greenberg & Goldman, 1988). Rogers noted that learning is most effective when it occurs experientially (e.g., within the context of a patient-therapist relationship), but he was the first to employ the more structured method of requiring students to record interviews for analysis and review during supervision.

Although inspired by Rogers (1957), Carkhuff (1969), Egan (1975), and Ivey (1971) all expanded on this work by developing more structured exercises aimed at promoting the ability of trainees to identify, and eventually acquire, very specific therapeutic skills. In this approach, particular interpersonal skills are translated into concrete behavioral activities that can be utilized in a group format. In contrast to the earlier approaches, these more recent techniques "strive to identify essential interpersonal skills and then teach these skills to group members through a sequence of modeling, practice, and feedback" (Zucker, Worthington, & Forsyth, 1985; p. 247). This emphasis on interpersonal skills has likely contributed to the identification of both Truax and Carkhuff's and Egan's techniques as "human relations training" (Toukmanian & Rennie, 1975). Although similar in structure in some ways, Ivey (1971) has identified his training strategy as "microcounseling" in order to stress the brief time period needed to implement this training model and the decreased emphasis on the necessity for an experiential component in the training.

In creating their didactic-experiential model of training, Truax and Carkhuff (1967) criticized previous therapist training models for relying too heavily on theory and patient psychodynamics. In contrast, Truax and Carkhuff argued that good therapists are skilled in building relationships with clients. Thus, they developed a program aimed at training potential therapists in interpersonal skills. This technique uses two phases of training. The first, or discrimination phase, consists of identifying the necessary therapeutic conditions (e.g., empathic understanding). Trainees listen to audiotaped recordings of counselor models and are taught to differentiate the levels of counselor communication described by Carkhuff and Pierce (1975). Accurate empathy is described as "understanding and sensing the other person and communicating this understanding to them" (Barak et al., 1988, p. 459). In addition to accurate empathy, the skills modeled on the audiotapes are nonpossessive warmth, genuineness, respect, concreteness, self-disclosure, challenging, and immediacy of the relationship. In the second phase, or communication training phase, trainees practice these new skills through role-plays. Role-plays are recorded and evaluated, and the trainee is encouraged to use higher levels of communication skills. Truax and Carkhuff (1967) concluded that approximately 100 hours of this type of training will result in performances at a level similar to that of experienced therapists.

Egan's (1975) training has many similarities to the Truax and Carkhuff (1967) model, and in fact, Egan credits them as being the "major influence" on his approach to counselor training. The "helper's skills" necessary for Egan's model are attending, accurate empathy, respect, genuineness, concreteness, self-disclosure, immediacy, challenge, alternative frames of reference, elaboration of action programs, and support. Egan notes that different skills are needed for different stages of the model. Accurate empathy is operationally defined as including the following skills: attending, listening, and reflecting. At Stage 1 (primary level) of the model, the helper is required to respond in a manner that demonstrates that s/he has both listened to and understood the client. Using the client's frame of reference, the helper must communicate this understanding to the client. At Stage 2 (advanced level) of accurate empathy, more subtle demonstrations of empathy are required. The helper must communicate an understanding of both verbal and implied statements from the client. The helper then points out associations between apparently unconnected statements made by the client. During this process, the helper is cautioned to reflect the client's message as accurately as possible.

Zucker et al. (1985) describe their empathy training program as based on Egan's model. Their training begins by providing candidates with a didactic overview of the skills needed for accurate empathy, as outlined by Egan (i.e., attending, listening, and reflecting), followed by a behavioral description of each skill. The trainees are then required to watch videotapes of negative and positive examples of each skill. Finally, using role-plays the trainees put into practice the skills they have viewed, followed by a discussion summarizing the results of the training. It should be noted that in both the Egan and Truax and Carkhuff models, the experiential component of practicing the skills within the context of a facilitative therapeutic relationship is considered essential.

Ivey's (1971) "microcounseling" approach differs from both the Truax and Carkhuff (1967) and Egan (1975) models in that Ivey maintains that counsellor skills, including empathy, can be taught in a relatively brief period (1-2 hrs) and that experiential learning is not necessary. Ivey (1973) reports that the "demystification process" is crucial to microcounseling in that the "mysterious skills of the counselor are clearly defined and presented in concrete, readily transmissible form" (p, 311). Egan Ivey notes that attending behavior is the "basic skill" of the microcounseling framework; although, he notes that other behaviors are also important to effective counseling. In fact, Ivey describes four skill clusters including 1) skills of the beginning counselor (attending behavior, open-ended questioning, minimal encouragement); 2) listening skills (reflection of feelings, paraphrasing, summarizing); 3) sharing skills (expression of feelings, interpretation of test scores, direct mutual communication); and 3) interpretation skills. More complex skills such as empathy are considered combinations of the above base skills (e.g., "attending skills help the beginning counselor give direction to natural empathy" Ivey, 1973; p.312).

In Ivey's approach, effective therapeutic skills are taught one at a time in a structured format. Ivey contends that previous approaches that taught several skills at the same time were confusing and overwhelming for the trainee. The format of microcounseling begins with either videotaping or audiotaping a five-minute counseling session between the trainee and a volunteer client. Following this first attempt at counseling, the trainee is provided with a written manual describing the single skill that is being taught and is exposed to a video or audio tape of an "expert" demonstrating the skill. The trainee then watches or listens to his own taped session and compares his own performance with that described in the manual and demonstrated by the expert. Finally, the trainee engages in a second five-minute counseling session which is taped, and the review process is repeated until the trainee has grasped the skill. Ivey emphasizes that the procedure should be supervised by a warm and empathic trainer. The entire procedure is said to take only 45 minutes to one hour. The two most important aspects of Ivey's training are the single skills emphasis and the videotaped observation.

Research supports the effectiveness of both the human relations method (Berenson, Carkhuff, & Myrus, 1966, Carkhuff & Griffin, 1971; Carkhuff, Kratochvil, & Friel, 1968, Perkins & Atkinson, 1973) and the microcounseling approach (Allen & Ryan, 1969; Higgins, Ivey, & Uhlemann, 1970; Mitchell, Rubin, Bozarth, & Wyrick, 1971; Moreland, Ivey, & Phillips, 1973; Toukmanian &

Rennie, 1975). However, the controversy over whether therapeutic skills are best taught purely didactically (Ivey, 1971) or whether they require an experiential component (Truax & Carkhuff, 1967) continues to be debated. Some theoreticians suggest that basic skills such as attending and summarization may be learned didactically but that higher level skills such as creating and maintaining an empathic relationship require experiential training (Greenberg & Goldman, 1988). Interestingly, however, Toukmanian and Rennie (1975) found that when they compared human relations training with microcounseling, both groups demonstrated significant improvements compared to a no training group. This was true on all of the therapist characteristics; although, the microcounseling subjects showed significantly greater gains in empathy. It appears, then, that a briefer didactic approach may be sufficient for teaching even subtle therapeutic skills.

Our therapeutic techniques training package (Fernandez et al., 2002) combines elements of the Truax and Carkhuff (1967), Egan (1975), and the Ivey (1973) approaches. Similar to Truax and Carkhuff, it is our view that an experiential component is beneficial to learning therapist skills; however, this training package may be delivered in a relatively brief period of time (e.g., four 6-hour days for a total of 24 hours of training). Additionally, it is our belief that an empathic relationship between the client and therapist is facilitated when the therapist understands the concept of empathy, is able to take the perspective of the client (e.g., understands what the client would perceive as empathic behavior), and demonstrates a broad range of positive therapeutic skills (e.g., attending, listening, and reflecting).

Similar to other training approaches, our training package includes both didactic and experiential components. Our empathy training section begins with a review of the research literature on the relationship between therapist empathy and positive treatment outcome. This section is meant to underscore the importance of empathy within the therapeutic environment. Varying definitions of empathy, including the Marshall, Hudson, Jones, and Fernandez (1995) stages of empathy, are then described. Finally, the trainer provides an overview of the therapeutic skills (e.g., open-ended questioning, reflective listening) shown to be related to positive outcome in the literature and underlines the importance of using these skills to develop an empathic relationship with clients (please note that a more extensive review, modeled demonstrations, and role-play practices of these skills have already been provided earlier in the training).

The experiential portion of the empathy training component includes both role-play and role-reversal techniques. Participants are divided into "therapy groups" of 8-10 members and take turns role-playing the therapist or the target client. The group members not role-playing a therapist or target client are required to role-play the other clients in the treatment group. Following a role-play as the therapist, each participant is then required to engage in a "role-reversal" in which they play the client until every participant has had an opportunity to role-play the therapist and the target client at least once.

In order to facilitate these role-plays, the group is provided with a mock empathy exercise (see section on training clients to be empathic for a description of empathy exercises by Marshall, O'Sullivan, & Fernandez, 1996), supposedly completed by the target client. The trainee therapists are required to role-play a session for 30 minutes, followed by 15 minutes of feedback. They are instructed to use all of the therapeutic skills they have been shown during the training to create an empathic relationship with both the client and other group members, model empathy appropriately, and encourage demonstrations of empathy in their group members. As described in Chapter 8, role-plays may be stopped during the session if a participant becomes distressed or the session appears to be going in an unproductive direction.

Following the role-play, a discussion is led by the trainer in which the trainee therapist is asked to evaluate how well s/he accomplished the goal of establishing an empathic relationship with his/her group members and describe what techniques s/he felt were particularly useful. The individual who role-played the target client is then asked the same questions, and finally, all group members are asked to contribute their perceptions and feelings about the session.

The evaluation of the person playing the target client as well as those playing the other group members is considered a crucial component of this empathy training component. As mentioned earlier in this chapter, research has suggested that clients may perceive the same display of empathy differently (Bachelor, 1988). As a result, we feel it is important to elicit feedback regarding the client's experience during the session. In addition, following a role-play as the therapist, each participant is then required to engage in a "role-reversal" in which s/he plays the client. Many participants have indicated that the role-reversal provides them with a different perspective of what "empathy" looks like to the client.

At the end of the complete training package (24 hours), each participant is rated by the trainer on the various skills that have been described as contributing to a positive, cohesive, and empathic therapeutic relationship. The Therapist Criteria scale is included in Appendix I of this chapter. Each skill is rated on a scale of 0,1, or 2, with 0 indicating the participant never demonstrated the skill or demonstrated the opposite of the skill, 1 indicating the participant was able to demonstrate the skill but not perfectly or consistently, and 2 indicating the participant consistently demonstrated the skill throughout the training. Total scores can range from 0 to 50. This training program has been used to train therapists working with sexual offenders at Her Majesty's Prison Service, running what is known as the "Rolling Programme" (a continuous intake group treatment program). The criteria that has been set for therapists in this training is a score of 46 for "Primary Therapists" and a score of 30 for "Secondary Therapists." Primary Therapists are participants who are considered very skilled and able to lead, direct, and make clinical decisions for a treatment group. Secondary Therapists are participants who demonstrate less sophistication or comfort with the skills included in the criteria. They are required to work with a Primary Therapist at all times who will provide them with continual feedback and encouragement as they develop their skills.

The therapist training techniques described above do not exhaust the list of suggested empathy training approaches described in the literature. Training in therapist empathy has included verbal instruction (Shaffer and Hummel, 1979), programmed instructions, and text structuring (Bender, 1973; Crabb, Moracco, & Bender, 1983; Kimberlin & Friesen, 1977), use of audiotaped or videotaped models (Berenson, 1971; Dalton, Sundblad, & Hylbert, 1973; Payne, Weiss, & Knapp, 1972; Perry, 1975; Stone & Vance, 1976), and role-playing (Guzetta, 1976; Stone & Vance, 1976). Other studies have examined whether individual or high level supervision, as compared to low level or group instructor involvement, is beneficial (Crabb et al., 1983; Hodge, Payne, & Wheeler, 1978).

It should be noted, however, that any study of empathy training programs may have serious limitations. First, as noted in Chapter 2 on the measurement of empathy, the difficulties in both defining and measuring empathy have resulted in a shortage of sound outcome measures (Kremer & Dietzen, 1991). Studies have either used self-report measures, written responses to vignettes (Crabb et al., 1983), or trait inventories such as Carkhuff's (1969) rating scale. Each of these methods of evaluation has its own limitations. Additionally, as Kremer and Dietzen (1991) note, few studies have investigated the long-term impact of empathy training programs, and there is some evidence to suggest that the effects of training diminish over time (Baker & Daniels, 1989).

Training Clients to Be Empathic

Links between empathy deficits and lifestyle problems have been documented for a variety of clinical populations. Poor empathy has been linked to aggressive behavior in both adults and children. Abusive parents and the children of abusive parents both show lower scores on empathy tests (Feshbach & Roe, 1968). It is suggested that low empathy skills contribute to poor interpersonal interactions and poor intimacy levels (see Chapter 6 on Emotional Expression and Recognition), and it has been shown that sexual offenders have lower levels of empathy than do other groups (Fernandez, Marshall, Lightbody, & O'Sullivan, 1999; Fernandez & Marshall, in press). Unfortunately, the majority of research on empathy training has relied on either "helping professionals," lay helpers, or university students as subjects; although, relatively more studies have described empathy training programs for children (D'Antonio, 1997; Feshbach, 1989; Kalliopuska & Tiitinen, 1991; Nicoletta, 2000).

For the most part, empathy training programs for clients have used the same methods as those used to train therapists. For example, both the Truax and Carkhuff (1967) and Ivey (1971) empathy training models have also been shown to increase interpersonal skills, including empathy skills, in psychiatric patients (Higgins et al., 1970; Pierce & Drasgow, 1969; Truax & Carkhuff, 1967). Cautela (1996) describes an empathy enhancement procedure for clients in which he provides both a definition of empathy and a theoretical model for empathy. Following an assessment of the client's empathy deficits, Cautela describes a series of behavioral procedures that include creating dissonance in the client by pointing out the differences between how he perceives his behavior and the responses of others (e.g., family members, colleagues, employers). Cautela then uses covert conditioning, positive reinforcement, modeling and role-plays (including role-reversal) in which the client has an opportunity to both identify and experience the effects of his own behavior. Finally, Cautela instructs the client to use his improved perspective-taking and empathy skills within his everyday life and report back to the therapist regarding the reactions of others. Feshbach's (1989) empathy training program for children includes activities such as problem-solving games, story-telling, listening to and making tape-recordings, written exercises, group discussions, and role-playing phrases and stories. Many of the exercises, particularly the role-plays, are videotaped and then replayed for discussion. During the exercises, the children are encouraged to act out their feelings and make guesses about the feelings of others. The are asked to experience and imagine themselves from various perspectives.

There are, in fact, numerous empathy training programs for clients described in the literature, but for the most part, the majority appear to include three main elements: a didactic component that involves instruction about the concept and definition of empathy; a component that attempts to improve the clients' ability to identify and label emotions in themselves and in others; and an experiential component in which clients are required to adopt the perspective of another person by "putting themselves in another's shoes." This often involves some type of role-play technique, including role reversal, although some programs use written exercises or discussion to accomplish the same goal. A review of the concept and various definitions of empathy are included in Chapter 1. Suggestions for aiding clients in the recognition and expression of emotions are described in Chapter 6, and role-play techniques for enhancing empathy are outlined in Chapter 8. As an example of an empathy enhancement program that uses these three strategies, we will now describe that component of our own treatment program.

The empathy enhancement component (see Marshall, O'Sullivan & Fernandez, 1996 for a detailed description) in our treatment program is one component of a more comprehensive cognitive-behavioral treatment program for sexual offenders (Marshall, Anderson, & Fernandez, 1999), which is run as a group therapy program involving 8-10 clients and two therapists. The focus of this component is to enhance offenders' empathy for their victims in particular and for others in general. In Chapter 1, we outlined our perspective of empathy, which involved the ability to accurately perceive the emotional state of another person (emotional recognition); the ability to see things as the other person sees them (perspective taking); the capacity to respond emotionally to the other person's distress (empathic responding); and finally, the enactment of some compassionate response (sympathy).

Our treatment component begins with a discussion of empathy in which program participants are encouraged to contribute their understanding of the concept of empathy. The therapist writes down each participant's ideas on a flip chart and, finally, adds our own definition of empathy for the group. The goal of this session is to have each participant leave with a better understanding of what empathy is and what skills they need to improve their own empathy. The second session is meant to improve participants' abilities to identify and label emotions in themselves and in others (emotional recognition). The walls of our treatment group room are decorated with laminated boards, depicting a wide range of emotions. Each board includes the written name of the emotion and a drawing depicting the emotion. Prior to this session, participants are instructed to look at the various boards and ask about any emotions they find unfamiliar. During this session, each offender is required to describe an emotionally distressing experience he has had during his life. The participants are encouraged to use a wide range of labels to describe their emotions. They are told that they can use the wall boards for help if they are struggling with their description. Each other group member is then required to offer their appraisal of the description and identify the target person's emotions and their own emotional responses. In order to emphasize the empathic responding stage of our empathy model, the therapist underlines how hearing a description of another person's distress evokes emotions in ourselves.

The perspective-taking aspect of our training program begins with a "brainstorming" session in which participants are asked to contribute possible effects that sexual assault has on victims (although not necessarily their own victim). The therapist writes all of the suggestions on a flip chart and adds any effects that are missed by the group. The list should include both short and long-term effects of sexual assault on victims. Next, each group member is required to identify which of the effects he thinks is relevant to his own victim. Each group member appraises the other's comments, and challenges are offered if an offender appears reluctant to accept that his victim has been negatively affected. Then each group member is required to describe their offense from the perspective of the victim, including the immediate and post-offense thoughts and feelings the victim might experience. Once again, members are challenged on their descriptions.

In a more experiential exercise, our clients are required to write a hypothetical letter, supposedly from the victim to themselves. The offender is instructed to write the letter as though he were the victim by putting himself "in the victim's shoes" (see Appendix II for a copy of the exercise instructions for both clients and therapist taken from Mann & Fernandez, 2001). The letter should reflect the anger, hurt, confusion, loss of trust, and guilt that the victim might feel as well as any other distress and behavioral problems s/he might experience. The letter should also be quite personalized and relevant to the specifics of the group member's particular offense so that it is not simply a list of "possible" effects. Each letter is read aloud to the group, and each group member is provided with an opportunity to comment on the letter and offer suggestions.

Some of our participants have demonstrated difficulty with understanding particular aspects of the victim's experience. For example, some group members struggle with the idea that the victim was negatively affected during the offense itself (e.g., they maintain the victim enjoyed the sexual activity). In contrast, other participants, while accepting that the offense produced a negative experience for the victim, maintain that the victim has "gotten over it" and has not been affected in the long-term. For these clients, we have an additional exercise (see Appendix III for a copy of the exercise instructions for both clients and therapist taken from Mann & Fernandez, 2001). Depending on the particular deficit, the group member is required to write a mock diary entry by his victim either from immediately after the offense (e.g., one hour later) or from a significant period following the offense (e.g., 10 years later). This exercise has several advantages over the victim letter. First, the exercise can be targeted to the specific deficits in the perspective-taking the client is demonstrating, and second, a mock diary entry has the advantage of being relatively "uncensored." That is, what someone would write in their diary might be significantly different from what they would write in a letter they anticipate will be read by another person. The diary entry exercise is then able to get around claims by the offender that his victim "would never say something like that to me." As with the other written exercise, these diary entries are read aloud within the group, and all group members provide feedback.

As a final exercise, group members are required to write a hypothetical letter back to the victim (see Appendix IV for a copy of the exercise instructions for both clients and therapist taken from Mann & Fernandez, 2001). In this letter, the offender should take responsibility for his behavior, legitimize the victim's feelings, express regret for his actions, and apologize for his behavior without asking for forgiveness. This exercise is meant to demonstrate the final stage of our definition of the empathic process, namely enactment of a compassionate or sympathetic response.

After this letter is read aloud to the group, the offender is asked to describe how he feels having now taken the perspective of the victim (empathic responding). Many of our group participants verbalize feelings of distress as well as relief at having the opportunity (even hypothetically) of apologizing for their behavior after coming to a better understanding of the victim's perspective.

The majority of clients that we treat demonstrate benefits from this empathy training component (Marshall, O'Sullivan, & Fernandez, 1996). For clients who continue to struggle with this section, we may require some additional exercises. In some cases, we may ask clients to describe a sexual assault on a well-loved family member (or current partner). He is to describe the sexual assault in sufficient detail to make it clear it was against the victim's will and was a distressful experience. He is then asked to describe the victim's suffering and his own feelings about the assault. Sometimes, this "personalization" of sexual assault is enough to break through the participant's resistance to taking the perspective of their victim. In some of the very challenging cases, we will use role-play and role-reversal techniques in order to provide the client with an opportunity to experience events from the victim's perspective. While these techniques are often very powerful, there are drawbacks to using role-plays, particularly when working with sexual offenders. Some of these problems are outlined in Chapter 8 on using role-play to enhance empathy. As a result, we reserve such role-play strategies for only the most resistant offenders, and they are implemented with very careful supervision.

CONCLUSIONS

There appears to be some evidence that empathy, similar to other interpersonal skills, can be effectively taught to both professionals and clients. Regardless of the definition of empathy used, most training programs include a didactic component that incorporates instruction and modeling and some type of experiential component (e.g., perspective-taking and role-playing). There is also evidence to suggest that empathy training may be successfully implemented in a relatively brief period of time (Ivey, 1973).

As mentioned at the beginning of this chapter, empathy has been described as "one of the most basic and necessary skills in human communication" (Barak et al. 1988, p. 458), whether in the context of a professional relationship or within personal relationships. Perhaps, then, it is not surprising that both professionals and clients appear to benefit from similar training techniques. Therapists should keep in mind, however, that this similarity in both the need for and ability to benefit from empathy training underscores the importance of adequate training for all "helping professionals" before they embark on empathy training for their clients. It is our view that the first step to teaching clients empathy is first to recognize, understand, and model empathy (Fernandez, 2001).

8

THE USE OF ROLE-PLAYS IN DEVELOPING EMPATHY

R. E. Mann, M. Daniels, & W. L. Marshall

"Good teaching is one-fourth preparation and three-fourths theatre."
Gail Godwin (1937-)

Elsewhere in this book, the rationale for developing empathy and perspective-taking skills with various clients has been fully explored and will not be repeated here. The use of role-play in the treatment of sexual offenders is predicated on the assumption that empathy for victims must be enhanced in the rehabilitation of these offenders. Treatment procedures aim not only at increasing empathy toward the offender's own victims but also enhancing the ability to generalize this empathy to future potential victims as well as improving more general interpersonal perspective-taking. Increased skill at interpersonal perspective-taking should improve the quality of intimate and social relationships, which are protective factors for future criminal activity particularly with violent or sexual offenders. Enhancement of social perspective-taking is seen as necessary in treating individuals who are prepared to hurt others in the pursuit of pleasure (e.g., Clarizio, 1987).

Role-Play Techniques

Role-play is commonly used in clinical interventions with offenders and is aimed at achieving the afore-mentioned goals (Morris & Braukmann, 1987). In fact, role-play techniques are in widespread use for a broad range of problems (Caballo, 1998). Given its popular use in psychological practice, it is perhaps surprising that so little has been written about the use of role-play with offenders. As noted, most of our work has primarily focused on using role-play techniques to enhance empathy.

The techniques described below do not constitute psychodrama or drama therapy (see Bergman, 1995, for a description of these approaches with sexual offenders). Rather, role-play techniques are rooted in cognitive-behavioral theory and practice, and we recommend their use within programs based on that theoretical model. In our view, experience with role-play facilitates the implementation of other cognitive-behavioral techniques such as cognitive restructuring, by allowing an individual in therapy to experience emotional reactions and to recognize these reactions in others. In this way, it is akin to other methods designed to enhance emotional awareness, such as evocative imagery (Dryden, 1987).

Role of the Therapist

To facilitate clear, concise, and effective role-plays, it is important for the therapists to control both the role-plays and the group at the same time. We use the descriptor "Director" to identify the position the therapist takes so that it is clear who is responsible for the action and direction of the role-play. The director is responsible for setting the scene, the time, and place of the role-play and for helping the participants with the roles they are playing. The director also plans the action in advance in a way that is consistent with the character of the client who is the target of the role-plays. It also the responsibility of the director to explain the purpose of the role-plays and to describe for the participants their respective roles. These instructions should be clear and concise.

A practice run will reveal to the director how well the participants have grasped their roles. Evidence from the practice run will indicate whether or not assistance is needed to maximize the reality of the role-play. At this point, the director may find it useful to model appropriate enactments of the roles. The director should ensure that no member of the treatment group makes fun of, or mocks, the role enactments, especially if they are somewhat clumsy. Any fears or anxieties either of the actors have should be allayed as far as possible before proceeding. It is best to periodically stop each role-play at the end of natural segments in order to allow discussion about what has gone on so far. This not only facilitates more realistic enactments, it also allows greater understanding by the target client of both his own actions, thoughts, and feelings, and those of the other person. Finally, at the end of each role-play session, the director is responsible for debriefing the participants and ensuring that their mood is stabilized after what can be a distressing experience.

Role-Plays

Role-plays allow the client either to behaviorally practice the skills he is being taught (e.g., assertiveness) or to practice roles so that he can gain insight into his thoughts and feelings or improve his ability to discern another person's perspective. Role-play has been used to modify a variety of skills such as improving the social skills of schizophrenics (Mueser, 1998), increasing assertiveness (Kazdin, 1980), modifing fighting among children (Martin & Pear, 1992), treating post-traumatic stress disorder (Cloitre, 1998), ameliorating depression (Beck, Rush, Shaw, &

Emery, 1979), and assessing the nature of the problems various clients present (Bellack & Hersen, 1998). In addition, role-plays have been employed with both juvenile (Gottshalk, Davidson, Mayer, & Gensheimer, 1987) and adult criminals (Platt & Prout, 1987) as well as with sexual offenders (Pithers, 1994). The focus of this chapter will be on the use of these techniques with sexual offenders where the goal is to enhance their empathy. Hopefully these illustrations will allow the readers (along with consulting the above-mentioned sources) to adapt the procedures to their own particular client group.

As Miller and Rollnick (1991) point out, "complex skills are not established without practice" (p. 160). They recommend role-plays as ways to practice skills that are being taught; however, role-plays also permit the person to recognize their thoughts and feelings and the thoughts and feelings of others, each of which is particularly relevant to developing empathy.

In role-plays, the client can play himself or another person, in fact, to maximize effectiveness, it is useful in most cases for clients to do both. When the client plays himself (which we will call "role-play of self"), it provides the opportunity for him to identify his thoughts and feelings as the role-enactment progresses. It also allows him to enact the behaviors he may have used when interacting with (or victimizing) another person in the absence of the rewarding or punishing consequences of his actions. This permits him to obtain a more objective evaluation of his behaviors. When the client switches roles to that of the other person (called "role reversal"), this allows him to see things from the other person's perspective and to recognize the emotional responses and thoughts that the other person will likely experience in response to his behaviors. These are the key elements of role-play techniques. In this chapter, we are concerned with the use of role-play to develop empathy and perspective-taking, so we, therefore, recommend that in such role-plays, a client be asked to take on the role of another. This may, for instance, be the role of someone he has actually victimized, or it may be the role of an imagined potential future victim.

In the following sections, we will describe some techniques that have been used and make recommendations for safe, effective role-play practice. Some sections will be based on our use of these techniques with sexual offenders to develop their empathy for victims, and other sections will be based on empathy enhancement components described in other programs (e.g., role-play of the self). These procedures and the goal for enhancing empathy are but one component in an otherwise comprehensive treatment approach (Mann & Thornton, 1998; Marshall, Anderson, & Fernandez, 1999).

Role-Play of Self

This descriptor refers to having the client play himself either enacting his offense or enacting an offense-related scenario. Hildebran and Pithers (1989) describe a role-play component to their program for enhancing victim empathy among sexual offenders. They had each offender "act out the concrete details of the offense" (p. 241) as the first step in this process. During the role-play employed in this program, the offender enacts the details of his actual offense and expresses aloud his ongoing thoughts and feelings. In Hildebran and Pithers' program, this role-play was videotaped for later review by the offender "to foster an accurate perception of his conduct" (Pithers, 1999, p. 271).

Care in conducting such role-plays is essential. First, it is not clear how far the role-plays should go in enacting every detail of the offense behaviors. Some of these behaviors might reinstate the deviant pleasures the offender experienced during his assaults, or they might arouse other group members. Both of these consequences would be counterproductive. Second, explicit enactments of the offense may distress an already vulnerable client to such an extent that he may not profit from the experience and may be unable to effectively participate thereafter. Pithers (1997) illustrates the ways in which these role-plays can go wrong. In his report on the use of these role-plays, Pithers notes that the therapists directing the re-enactments went too far in graphically recreating the offenses, causing extreme distress to the clients, which resulted in the launching of a civil suit against the program. Thus, if a decision is made to use these role-plays, great care must be taken to establish the boundaries or limits to the details that are re-enacted. Certainly, direct physical contacts should be avoided, or if they are used at all, the contacts should be symbolic; for example, it could be agreed in advance that a light touch to the leg would symbolize penetration. As noted, the use of graphic re-enactments of offenses may trigger deviant sexual thoughts in the other group participants. This may either distress them or revive their dormant deviant fantasies, neither of which are desirable responses.

In an appraisal of our use of role-play enactments of the clients' offenses, we (Webster, Bowers, Mann, & Marshall, 2002) compared changes in empathy between groups of sexual offenders who either did or did not engage in offense re-enactments. The results indicated that some of those who role-played their offense showed slightly greater improvements on an empathy measure than did those who did not enact their offense. However, the latter group showed greater understanding of the disruptive effects on their victims in the longer term. As a result of these observations, it may be concluded that the potential problems associated with offense re-enactments (see Pithers, 1997) are too great, and the potential benefits so few, that these role-plays may not be worth the risk. As an alternative, re-enactments of the offense in role-plays may be limited to only those cases where progress is otherwise stalled. For example, there are times when the client is having extreme difficulty understanding (or accepting) the distress that the victim experienced during the offense. This will limit his capacity to recognize current and subsequent harm. In those cases, it may be useful to have him role-play himself during a re-enactment that is limited to just those elements that most likely distressed the victim (e.g., having the offender say threatening things or having the offender wield a mock weapon). In addition, since people other than the victim are also affected by a sexual assault, it may be useful to have the offender enact role-plays with some or all of these other people. For example, the victim's family will be distressed by the assault and so will the offender's own family. In fact, for particularly intractable offenders, it may be best to begin with a role-play involving a distressed member of his own family. This experience may sensitize him to the more general suffering his actions have caused, and this may make it easier for him to acknowledge harm to his victim. It should be noted, however, that offense re-enactment is a controversial technique, which is difficult to control, open to misuse if therapists are not clear about their purpose (Pithers, 1997), and could potentially lead to a traumatic experience for the offender in treatment. Its use, therefore, leaves therapists open to criticism, and we do not recommend it as a technique. In fact, we typically only use role-reversal strategies. We believe that role-reversal enactments are the most effective component, and in almost all cases, this is all that is needed.

Role-Reversal

Our primary goal in using role-plays in our empathy component is to have the offender understand the thoughts and feelings of (i.e., take the perspective of) the victim. To achieve this goal, we believe role-playing himself committing the offense is, at best, no more than a preliminary step in the process.

Role-reversal (Lazarus, 1968) requires the client to take on the role of another person, and he is asked to think the other's thought and experience the other's feelings while enacting the other person's behaviors. Another person (usually the therapist, but we have also used other group members) enacts the role of the targeted client. This procedure enables the client to see his own behavior from another perspective (Fow, 1998). Pertinent to our use of this technique, the use of role-reversal alone has been shown to enhance empathic communication in marital partners (e.g., Fow, 1998; Long, Angera, Carter, Nakamoto, & Kalso, 1999). These findings encouraged us to believe that role-reversal strategies might be useful in encouraging the development of empathy among our sexual offending clients without the necessity of the prior step of having the offender play himself.

Role-reversal is facilitated by first having the person practice the role by asking him mundane questions as if he is the other person. For example, if a client were to play his victim, Karen, then we would ask him questions such as "How old are you, Karen?"; "What are you dressed in today, Karen?"; "What color is your hair, Karen?" He is encouraged to reply, as if he were Karen, using descriptions as rich in detail as possible. It is important that the client answer these questions in the first person (e.g., "I am 29 years old. I am wearing faded jeans and a red t-shirt."). If the client answers in the third person (e.g., "She has long blonde hair.") he should be corrected by instructing him, "No, you are Karen, what color is your hair today?"

If the client is enacting the role of a child, it is helpful to address questions in the manner you would use when talking to a child, for example, by using more simple, concrete language. It is also useful to ask questions that focus on the kinds of topics a child of that age would be interested in (e.g., sports, school, favorite games, best friends). It may be necessary to ask upwards of a dozen questions to help an individual adopt the role. Also note that some people adopt roles more readily than others. When the client is able to quickly and easily respond to questions about the person he is role-playing, then the role-reversal can begin.

In role-reversal the client may play the victim in a variety of roles. He may respond to a re-enactment of some aspects of the offense, or he may role-play a scene where he (i.e., the victim) is speaking to another person about how he or she was affected by the crime. In either case, the client adopts the role of his victim. This provides the client with the opportunity to be on the receiving end of his own responses. In effect, he is able to listen to, and then answer, his own statements. The person in the other role should be familiar with the client and should have seen the earlier role-play if there was one so that s/he can believably portray what the offender would say in the "real world."

While clients are enacting a role-play, the therapist should freeze the action periodically and ask the role-playing client to describe the current thoughts and feelings of the person they are playing (this process is called "thought-tracking"). This encourages the client to enter the role more effectively and assists him/her in developing insight into the perspective of his/her victim.

General Features

Most clients will never have encountered role-play before. The director should, therefore, set the boundaries with the help of the group before entering into any action. Within our programs for imprisoned sexual offenders, we have developed the following guidelines in order to ensure that all role-play work is conducted in a professional and safe way for our clients.

Before planning or carrying out a role-play exercise, ensure that your goal has been properly defined. The primary goal of role-plays in our program is to enhance the participants' understanding of the view their victims have of the offender's assaultive behaviors. For each individual case, this goal should be made more specific in accordance with the areas where he particularly lacks awareness of the impact of his offense. For instance, one offender might indicate that his victim "will have gotten over it by now," in which case an appropriate role-play would be set in the future and would involve a goal about developing his understanding of the long term impact of the offense. Another offender might believe that no one, other than his direct victim, had been affected, in which case a suitable goal would be to explore the impact of the offense on others close to the victim such as his/her own family members. In other programs there will be different goals (e.g., developing specific behavioral skills). Whatever the goals are, they should be clearly articulated to all concerned prior to initiating any role-plays.

Role-plays work by allowing participants to see the world and certain experiences from the perspective of another person. For example, role-plays can be used to develop victim empathy by allowing offenders to take the perspective of their victims or the perspective of others who are affected by the offense (e.g., the client's own family or the victim's family).

Preparation for Role-Plays

Preparation for role-play sessions is crucial. No role-play should be enacted that has not been carefully planned in advance. The plan should include identification of the goal of the role-play, the scenario in which the role-play will be set, the techniques to be used, the potential pitfalls and how they can be avoided, the role that each person (both the role enactors and the rest of the treatment group) will take, and how the participants will be debriefed.

Specifically, we recommend that in this preparation, it should be made clear that physical contact will be, at most, limited to symbolic gestures. As we have seen, Pithers (1997) describes the potential problems that may arise when physical contacts become too explicit within role-plays. Given the nature of sexual offending, offensive-specific physical contacts between role-play actors could border on abuse.

Also, there is no value in shocking or surprising participants during role-plays. Such surprises are likely to alienate clients and will, at the very least, result in role-play disruptions. Participants should agree in advance to everything that will take place within a role-play. Do not introduce sudden elements into a role-play such as surprising sounds or props not previously mentioned. The role-play should have a clear beginning and end, and activity should be strictly confined within these boundaries.

Stops in Role-Plays

It should be made clear that stops will occur. When the director instructs the participants to stop, they should understand that they must do so immediately so that the issue of concern can be discussed. The stops permit "thought tracking," a procedure that requires the participants to articulate their thoughts and feelings at specific points in the role-play. They can also be used to have the client identify the thoughts and feelings of his fellow actor.

Stopping role-plays can also serve to terminate unanticipated distress in the client. Sometimes when a client is role-playing either himself or his victim, he may suddenly become acutely aware of the harmful effects of his actions, and this may upset him. It is proper to stop the role-play when this happens, not to attenuate his distress but rather to have him describe why he is distressed. Of course, stopping a role-play may be done for various other reasons such as the role-play going off topic or the participants or observers not taking it seriously.

Selection of the Other Participant

Role-plays involve two characters, and it is essential that both understand their roles. The person who plays the role opposite to the target client must know the client and his problem well enough to effectively enact the role. The other character can make or break a role-play simply by the way in which he enacts his role. It is best to use other treatment clients whenever possible as this assists group cohesion. However, there may be occasions when having the therapist take the other role will be most effective. For example, there may not be anyone in the group who knows the target client well enough or who can enact the role sufficiently. In these cases, the therapist may enact the role in order to model what is required, whereas, in the former case, the therapist may have to take over the role.

Ending a Role-Play

Always finish a role-play by thought-tracking the participant through the experience as a whole. This involves having the client describe the thoughts and feelings he was experiencing as well as what thoughts and feelings the other person would be experiencing. To do this, it is best to have the client stay in role while the director speaks to him. Other group members should be required to ask questions of the participant to ensure that they are actively involved in order to maximize vicarious learning. After each role-play, the participants should be de-roled. De-roling involves bringing the participant back to the here and now by asking him to talk about who and where he is, then asking further questions to help him separate the person he is from the "role" he was playing. For example, the participant might be asked to talk about his plans for the rest of the day.

Next, a post role-play debrief is crucial, as it facilitates the client's enduring understanding of what he has learned. This debrief enables him to comment on the experience he had in the role and what he has learned from it. We want to know how he sees the role-played event differently as a result of taking a different perspective. The following prompts help the client integrate his experience: "Tell me what you have learned about yourself and the other person from the role-play." "What did you and the other person experience in that particular situation?" and "What effects did your behavior have on the other person?"

After the participant has had the opportunity to discuss the experience of taking another person's perspective, the group is invited to provide feedback based on their observations. In this respect, it helps to ask each group member to describe his own reactions and feelings about the role-play.

A Case Example

In this example, we describe the use of role-play with Alexander, a man who was convicted of raping a female colleague from work. Alexander had an influential and collusive group of friends who would visit him in prison and regale him with tales of how they had seen this woman out in bars and clubs around town apparently enjoying herself. Alexander used this information to argue in group that the victim had clearly not been affected at all by his offense against her. The goal of the role-play intervention, therefore, was set "to allow Alexander to explore how the victim could still be experiencing distress from the offense, even if her social life was active." The role-play goal was fully shared with Alexander beforehand, and he agreed that he would be interested to explore this issue, even though he indicated clearly that he did not see how any negative impact could be present.

Alexander was asked to take the role of the victim, Sally, preparing for a night out with her friends. Considerable time was spent helping Alexander into the role, which included some discussion of the offense she had endured a year previously. During this part of the role-play, Alexander acknowledged (as Sally) that she felt some discomfort and suspicion about men's motives in being nice to her. As this role-play took place within a therapy group, other group members were recruited to act as Sally's friends. With some guidance from the role-play director, Sally's friends encouraged her to dress up, go out, and have a few drinks because "It will help you feel better about yourself."

The role-play scene was then changed, and Alexander was asked to consider himself as Sally in a nightclub. Sally's friends were encouraging her to "let herself go" and accept a dance with another man. As Sally, Alexander refused the offer of dancing. The director paused the role-play at this point to use thought-tracking: "Why did Sally not want to dance?" As Sally, Alexander replied that he felt uncomfortable about what the man thought of her and what his intentions might be.

While Sally was sitting alone in the nightclub, another group member was recruited to play a friend of Alexander. He approached Sally and made some slightly insulting comments, suggesting that she was promiscuous and that she should not be enjoying herself after she had "put Alexander in prison." At this point, Alexander in role as Sally was unable to reply. Again thought-tracking was used, and Alexander indicated that he was experiencing considerable misery and distress as Sally. The director asked Sally what she would like to reply to Alexander's friend. As Sally, Alexander replied that she couldn't think of a reply, all she wanted to do was "go home and hide under my duvet." At this point, the role-play was ended, and Alexander engaged in a discussion with his therapists and the other group members about some of the unexpected thoughts and feelings he had experienced while taking the role of Sally.

It should be noted that this was a hypothetical situation and not one which (to the therapists' knowledge) had actually occurred. It is our view that real-life situations are more tricky to examine in role-play. However, the situation chosen was realistic and possible, and it was specifically tailored to Alexander's own beliefs and lifestyle. This role-play was remarkably effective for Alexander; he frequently referred to it throughout the remainder of his treatment as a turning point. Also, following this treatment session, he showed a zeal, hitherto not remotely apparent, for discussing and identifying the perspectives of other people and also used this newfound skill to advise and guide other group members.

DEALING WITH PROBLEMS

When inappropriate laughter occurs, it is important to remind the group of the purpose of the role-plays. This is especially important when using role-play to develop empathy for others. If an individual group member is apparently finding the session amusing, then it is important to stop the role-play and address the issue. Such laughter may be a defense or a sign of resistance to addressing difficult or uncomfortable topics, and this should be discussed within the group.

Apparent Sexual Arousal During Role-Plays

If you are working with sexual offenders, it is possible that the observing or participating group members might become sexually aroused during a role-play. While this happens rather infrequently, it must be addressed if and when it does occur. As noted earlier, we have circumscribed our actual enactments of offenses in order to reduce this possibility. If the therapist believes a group member is becoming sexually aroused while participating in, or observing, a role-play, the action should be stopped. The apparent signs of arousal should be described and discussed and a resolution reached before proceeding any further.

Dealing with Distress

Sometimes participants in a role-play become distressed. When this is apparent, the role-play should be stopped. The client should then be asked about his experience in the role-play to find out whether it has put him in touch with something in his own past or present life that needs to be addressed. Sometimes this distress is the result of the role-play making the client aware of the harm he has caused others. Sometimes it reminds a client of the facts concerning his own victimization. In either case, he should be encouraged to talk about his experience and what happened to him. It is necessary to determine which part of the role-play most affected him. Therapists should reassure the participant and offer him support both in the group and after the session is finished. Under no circumstances should a distressed client be pressured to continue with the role-play.

Ensuring Safe Practice

The techniques described above can lead to strong emotional responses from group members, which can be cathartic and helpful, but these responses need to be skilfully managed. We recommend that any therapists using role-play techniques should ensure that their work is monitored and supervised by an objective and experienced colleague. Pithers (1997) notes that inadequate supervision of role-plays allowed them to drift in an inappropriate and harmful direction.

When properly supervised, therapists are able to utilize and employ their skills to ensure effective and professional service delivery. The effectiveness of their techniques is maximized, and the danger of unethical or unprofessional practice is minimized through supervision. Therapists should be monitored to ensure they are always treating their clients with respect and are working with the client's best interests at heart. Role-play work has the potential to become abusive, particularly when working to develop victim empathy or when working with incarcerated clients who feel they have little choice about their participation (Pithers, 1997). Supervision can minimize these potential dangers.

CONCLUSIONS

Our recommendations for incorporating role-play safely into treatment programs for offenders include the techniques and their use should be specified in sufficient detail in a manual so that therapists know what is expected of them and what is not permitted; therapists using role-play techniques should be properly trained in those techniques or should initially work with more experienced therapists; role-plays should be supervised by a senior person whose role is clearly distinct from that of the therapist and who is committed to ensuring safe practice and treatment integrity; finally, this supervisor should be easily accessible to the therapists.

Appendix I

Criteria for Therapist Assessment

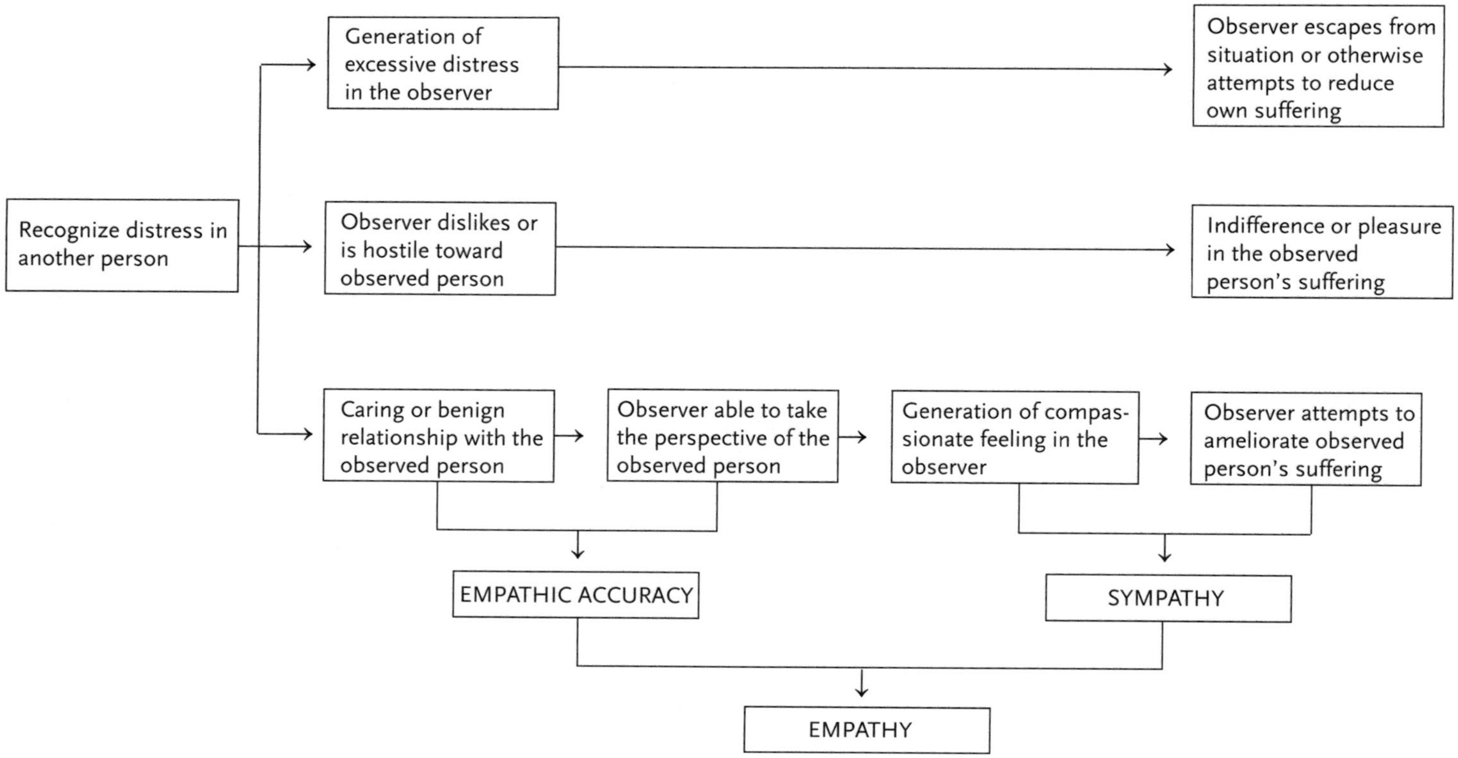

Appendix II

CRITERIA FOR THERAPIST ASSESSMENT

Name:_____

Assessor & Date:_____

Criterion	Opposite Behaviors	Score 0/1/2
1. Can they effectively use reinforcement within the session? Effective = appropriate, sincere, specific, relevant, contingent, regular	Failing to use reinforcement or using it ineffectively Ineffective = vague, non-contingent, insincere, inappropriate, poor timing, distracting	
2. Do they provide opportunities for success?	Trying to trip people up or trap them into corners	
3. Do they allow discussions to take a natural course while maintaining a guiding hand?	Clamping discussions down; allowing group to get out of control	
4. Can they select the most relevant issues for feedback?	Giving too much feedback at one time; giving trivial feedback	
5. Are they aware of group process and able to adjust to it?	Not noticing group process issues; focusing on content noticeably more than process; seeming uncomfortable with displays of emotions or expressions of negative views within the group	
6. Do they respond to group members' emotions properly?	Failing to acknowledge emotions, ridiculing or ignoring emotions, seeming uncomfortable with emotions	
7. Can they handle and use opportunities arising in the group?	Rigidly sticking to a schedule, ignoring or not identifying opportunities that could be used for learning	

Criterion	Opposite Behaviors	Score 0/1/2
8. Do they understand the theory of sex offender treatment and understand what makes a good assignment?	Unable to pick out good and bad aspects of an assignment, distracted by red herrings unrelated to sexual offending, fails to notice factors related to sexual offending	
9. Are they aware of their personal issues and have they addressed them sufficiently to prevent their work being affected?	Unaware of personal issues, unwilling to acknowledge personal issues, distracted or distressed by personal issues, personal emotions or issues leaking out through verbal or non-verbal language	
10. Are they using optional exercises appropriately? For example, do they seem to know what thought exercise to suggest after an assignment?	Miss opportunities to use optional exercises, not noticing needs that could be met through an optional exercise, prescribing optional exercises when not needed	
11. Do they know when to end an exercise or discussion?	Ending exercises or discussions too early or too late	
12. Do they appropriately emphasize change and helping people, rather than disclosure as a main goal?	Emphasizing disclosure as a main goal; turning non-disclosure exercises into disclosures	
13. Do they seem like a helpful member of the group? Do they work with the group at their level although maintaining an appropriate professional relationship?	Seeming like a distant authoritarian figure or as if trying to be friends with group members	
14. Do they know their aims at all times and accomplish them while still being flexible?	Not sure where to go with an exercise or how to achieve their aims	
15. Do they have a warm style? Do they seem to like their group members?	Formal, distant, seeming to dislike individual group members	

Criterion	Opposite Behaviors	Score 0/1/2
16. Do they seem non-judge-mental of their group members, able to accept them as they are?	Hostile, judgemental about offenders or offending, seeming to dislike sexual offenders as a group	
17. Are they able to challenge appropriately in terms of being challenging but not confrontational?	Too confrontational or too non-confrontational, letting things go or being collusive	
18. Are they good models? Do they model and encourage anti-criminal attitudes and behaviors?	Missing opportunities to model anti-criminal attitudes/behavior; missing opportunities to reward anti-criminal attitudes/behavior; failing to explicitly encourage anti-criminal attitudes/behavior	
19. Are they motivational in the way they present their feedback e.g. referring to "areas for change" instead of "problems"?	Present feedback in a way that implies failure or poor performance, referring to "problems" or "shortcomings" in someone's work, communicating lack of respect for someone's work, focusing on problems more than achievements	
20. Are they respectful toward both co-therapists and group members?	Cutting people off, dominating the group, using sarcasm, appearing condescending	
21. Do they show appropriate body language? Do they appear open and interested in their body language?	Closed, negative body posture: arms crossed, legs crossed, eyes closed, clipboard on their lap, behind a desk	
22. Do they appear to be confident and comfortable as therapists?	Nervous, hesitant, unsure	

Criterion	Opposite Behaviors	Score 0/1/2
23. Are they a clear communicator? Do they express their meaning clearly and succinctly/concisely?	Rambling, making questions more complex and confusing than they need to be, asking more than one question in a sentence, not getting to their point	
24. Do they use humor when appropriate?	Inappropriate use of humor e.g. sexual jokes, presenting as very humorless.	
25. Have they participated fully in the training?	Lack of participation in personal exercises or group discussions. Over-participation that excludes others from opportunities	

Primary Therapists: Must score at least 46/50.
                           No zero scores allowed.
                           Maximum of four 1-scores.

Secondary Therapists: Must score at least 40/50.
                           Five zero scores allowed.

You may gain access to and download this form in pdf format by visiting www.woodnbarnes.com. Enter ITS in the password field. (Adobe Acrobat Reader© is required to open the file.)

"Criteria for Therapist Assessment" used with permission of HM Prison Service, SOTP Rolling Programme.

Appendix III

Assignment Description

You are asked to imagine yourself as your victim or one of your victims (the group and facilitators will help you decide who this should be). If this person was to write you a letter today, what might they want to say to you? Try to write the letter that they might write. Remember to address this letter to yourself.

Guidance for Facilitators

Aim: To have group members demonstrate their understanding of the probable short term and long term effects of their abuse.

After an assignment has been read to the group, there is an opportunity for a good general discussion. Facilitators may need to begin the discussion by giving their own feedback first. You should give as feedback all the positives you can possibly think of and explain why everything you are praising was good.

The kinds of questions that you can use to get the group going with their own feedback include "What did you like about the letter?" and "What do you think could be improved about the letter?"

Appendix IV

ASSIGNMENT DESCRIPTION

You are asked to imagine yourself as your victim or as one of your victims (the group and facilitators will help you decide who this should be). If this person was to hear today that you are about to be released, what might they write in their diary? Try to write the diary entry that they might write.

Alternative: write the diary entry that you as the victim might have written the day after the offense.

Alternative: write the diary entry that you as the victim might have written on the anniversary of the offense (one year after it happened).

GUIDANCE FOR FACILITATORS

The aim of this exercise is for the group member to develop empathy for the victim's experience at a particular stage. It can be used flexibly depending on the particular empathy deficits of the group member. For instance, a group member who has a good understanding of immediate and short term effects may gain value from writing a diary entry for the anniversary or for the present day.

Appendix V

Write a letter as if you are writing to your victim (the group and facilitators will help you decide who to write to). What do you want to say to this person? What do you think you should say? What do they need to hear from you? Try and write the letter.

GUIDANCE FOR FACILITATORS

Aims: • For group members to demonstrate their understanding of short term and long term effects for their victim;
 • For group members to demonstrate that they take responsibility for their offense;
 • For group members to develop the skill of perspective-taking by putting themselves in the shoes of the person receiving the letter and thinking about how it would feel to read the letter;
 • For group members to recognise ongoing attempts they might make to control the victim/others.

When the letter has been read out by one of the facilitators, ask the group member who wrote it what he thinks it would feel like for the victim to read it. This can lead into a discussion about what victims would want to hear and what they would not care about. (There are no right answers to these questions but useful learning should take place during discussion). For example,

 • What might your victim feel about knowing you are in treatment? Would they care?
 • What might your victim feel about you suggesting she goes for counseling? Would they see this as a caring suggestion?
 • What might your victim feel on hearing that she is not responsible for the abuse?

Frame your questions around the content of the specific letter. Get the group to generate possible options in response to each question.

References

Abracen, J. A., Looman, J. A. & Anderson, D. (2000). Alcohol and Drug Abuse in Sexual and Nonsexual Violent Offenders. *Sexual Abuse: A Journal of Research and Treatment, 12*, 263-274.

Abraham, K. G., Kuehl, R. O., & Christopherson, V. A. (1983). Age-specific influence of parental behaviors on the development of empathy in preschool children. *Child Study Journal, 13*, 175-185.

Adams, G.R., Schvaneveldt, J.D., & Jenson, G.O. (1979). Sex, age and perceived competency as correlates of empathic ability in adolescence. *Adolescence, 12*, 811-818.

Ainsworth, M. D. (1963). The development of infant-mother interaction among the Ganda. In B. Foss (Ed.), *Determinants of Infant Behavior, Vol. 2*, pp. 114-138. New York: Wiley.

Ainsworth, M.D.S. (1973). The development of infant-mothers attachment. In B.M. Caldwell & H.N. Ricciuti (Eds). *Review of child development research, 111*, (pp. 1-94). Chicago: University of Chicago Press.

Allen, D., & Ryan, K. (1969). *Microteaching. Reading*, MA: Addison-Wesley.

Allport, F.H. (1924). *Social psychology.* Boston: Houghton Mifflin.

Andrews, D.A., Wormith, J.S., Daigle-Zinn, W.J., Kennedy, D.J., & Nelson, S. (1980). Low and high functioning volunteers in group counseling with anxious and non-anxious prisoners: The effects of interpersonal skills on group process and attitude change. *Canadian Journal of Criminology, 22*, 443-456.

Annis, H.M., & Chan, D. (1983). The differential treatment model: empirical evidence from a personality typology of adult offenders. *Criminal Justice and Behavior, 10*, 159-173.

Aronfreed, J. (1968). *Conduct and conscience: The socialization of internalized control over behavior.* New York: Academic Press.

Aronfreed, J. (1970). The socialization of altruistic and sympathetic behavior: Some theoretical and experimental analyses. In J. Macaulay & L. Berkowitz (Eds). *Altruism and helping behavior* (pp. 1-40). New York: Academic Press.

Asch, S.E. (1946). Forming impressions of personality. *Journal of Abnormal and Social Psychology, 41*, 248-290.

Bachara, G. H., Raphael, J., & Phelen, W. J. (1980). Empathy development in preadolescents. *American Annals of the Deaf, 125*, 38-41.

Bachelor, A. (1988). How clients perceive therapist empathy: A content analysis of "received" empathy. *Psychotherapy, 25*, 227-240.

Bachrach, H.M. (1976). Empathy: We know what we mean, but what do we measure? *Archives of General Psychiatry, 33*, 35-38.

Baker, S.B., & Daniels, T.G. (1989). Integrating research on the microcounseling program: A meta-analysis. *Journal of Counseling Psychology, 36*, 231-222.

Baldwin, J.M. (1897). *Social and ethical interpretations in mental development: A study in social psychology.* New York: Macmillan.

Bandura, A. (1977). Self-efficacy: Toward a unifying theory of behavior change. *Psychological Review, 84*, 191-215.

Barak, A., Engle, C., Katzir, L., & Fisher, W.A. (1988). Increasing the level of empathic understanding by means of a game. *Simulation and Games, 18*, 459-470.

Barbaree, H. E. (1991). Denial and minimization among sex offenders: Assessment and treatment outcome. *Forum on Corrections Research, 3*, 30-33.

Barnes, M. L., & Sternberg, R. J. (1989). Social intelligence and decoding of nonverbal cues. *Intelligence, 13*, 263-287.

Barnett, M.A., Howard, J.A., King, L.M., & Dino, G.A. (1981). Helping behavior and the transfer of empathy. *Journal of Social Psychology, 115*, 125-132.

Baron, R. A., & Richardson, D. R. (1994). *Human aggression* (2nd ed.). New York: Plenum Press.

Barrett-Lennard, G.T. (1962). Dimensions of therapist responses as causal factors in therapeutic change. *Psychological Monographs, 76* (43, Whole No. 562).

Barrett-Lennard, G.T. (1981). The empathy cycle: Refinement of a nuclear concept. *Journal of Counseling Psychology, 28*, 91-100.

Batson, C.D. (1987). Prosocial motivation: Is it ever truly altruistic. In L. Berkowitz (Ed). *Advances in experimental social psychology* (Vol. 20) (pp. 65-122). New York: Academic Press.

Batson, C.D., Duncan, B. D., Ackerman, P., Buckley, T., & Birch, K. (1981). Is empathic action a source of altruistic motivation? *Journal of Personality and Social Psychology, 40,* 290-302.

Batson, C.D., Fultz, J., & Schoenrade, P.A. (1987). Distress and empathy: Two qualitatively distinct vicarious emotions with different motivational consequences. *Journal of Personality, 55,* 19-39.

Batson, C.D., O'Quin, K., Fultz, J., Vanderplas, M., & Isen, A. M.(1983). Influence of self-reported distress and empathy on egoistic versus altruistic motivation to help. *Journal of Personality and Social Psychology, 45,* 706-718.

Beck, A. T. (1988). *Love is never enough.* New York, NY: Harper & Row Publishers.

Beck, A. T., Rush, J., Shaw, B., & Emery, G. (1979). *Cognitive therapy for depression.* New York: Guilford Press.

Beckett, R.C., Beech, A.R., Fisher, D., & Fordham, A.S. (1994). *Community-based treatment for sex offenders. An evaluation of seven treatment programs.* London: Home Office Publications Unit.

Beckett, R., & Fisher, D. (1994, November). *Assessing victim empathy: A new measure.* Paper presented at the 13th Annual Research and Treatment Conference of the Association for the Treatment of Sexual Abusers. San Francisco.

Beech, A. & Fordham, A. S. (1997). Therapeutic climate of sexual offender treatment programs. *Sexual Abuse: A Journal of Research and Treatment, 9,* 219-237.

Bell, S. M., & Ainsworth, M. D. (1972). Infant crying and maternal responsiveness. *Child Development, 43,* 1171-1190.

Bellack, A. S., & Hersen, M. (1998). *Behavioral assessment: A practical handbook* (4th ed.). Boston: Allyn & Bacon.

Bender, R.C. (1973). A comparative analysis of the short term and long term effects of didactic and programmed empathy training (Doctoral dissertation, University of Maine at Orono) *Dissertation Abstracts International, 34,* 7530A.

Berenson, B.G., Carkhuff, R.R., & Myrus, P. (1966). The interpersonal functioning and training of college students. *Journal of Counseling Psychology, 13,* 441-446.

Berenson, D.H. (1971). The effects of systematic human relations training upon classroom performance of elementary school student teachers. *Journal of Research and Development in Education, 11,* 70-85.

Bergman, J. (1995). Life, the life event, and theatre: A personal narrative on the use of drama therapy with sex offenders. In B. K. Schwartz & H.R. Cellini (Eds.). *The sex offender: Corrections, treatment and legal practice* (pp. 17.2 - 17.24). Kingston, NJ: Civic Research Institute.

Bernadett-Shapiro, S., Ehrensaft, D., & Shapiro, J. L. (1996). Father participation in childcare and the development of empathy in sons: An empirical study. *Family Therapy, 23,* 77-93.

Binet, A., & Simon, T. (1905). Methodes nouvelles pour le diagnostic du nivau intellectual des anormaux. *Annee Psychologique, 11,* 191-244.

Bischof-Koehler, D. (2000). Empathy, prosocial behavior and security of attachment in two-year-olds. *Psychologie in Erziehung und Unterricht, Vol 47.*

Bjorkqvist, K., Lagerspetz, K. M. J., & Kaukiainen, A. (1992). Do girls manipulate and boys fight? Developmental trends regarding direct and indirect aggression. *Aggressive Behavior, 18,* 117-127.

Bjorkqvist, K., & Niemela, P. (1992). New trends in the study of female aggression. (Eds.), *Of mice and women: Aspects of female aggression* (pp. 3-16). San Diego: Academic Press.

Bjorkqvist, K., Osterman, K., & Hjelt-Back, M. (1994). Aggression among university employees. *Aggressive Behavior, 20,* 173-184.

Bjorkqvist, K., Osterman, K., & Kaukiainen, A. (1992). The development of direct and indirect aggressive strategies in males and females. In K. Bjorkqvist & P. Niemela (Eds.), *Of mice and women: Aspects of female aggression,* (pp. 51-54). San Diego: Academic Press.

Bjorkqvist, K., Osterman, K., & Kaukiainen, A. (2000). Social intelligence – empathy = aggression? *Aggression and Violent Behaviour: A Review Journal, 5,* 191-200.

Bjorkqvist, K., Osterman, K., & Lagerspetz, K. M. (1994). Sex differences in covert aggression among adults. *Aggressive Behavior, 20,* 27-33.

Blaine, B., & Crocker, J. (1993). Self-esteem and self-serving biases in reactions to positive and negative events: An integrative review. In R.F. Baumeister (Ed.), *Self-esteem: The puzzle of low self-regard* (pp. 55-85.). New York, NY: Plenum.

Blum, L.A. (1980). *Friendship, altruism and morality.* London: Routledge & Kegan Paul.

Bowlby, J. (1969). *Attachment and Loss: Vol. 1. Attachment.* New York: Basic Books.

Bowlby, J. (1973). *Attachment and Loss: Vol. 2. Separation: Anxiety and Anger.* New York: Basic Books.

Bowlby, J. (1976). Human personality development in an ethological light. In G. Serban & A. Kling (Eds.) (1976). *Animal models in human psychobiology* (pp. 27-36). New York: Plenum.

Bowlby, J. (1980). *Attachment and Loss: Vol. 3. Loss, Sadness, and Depression.* New York: Basic Books.

Brehm, S.S. (1992). *Intimate relationships* (2nd Ed.). New York: McGraw-Hill.

Bretherton, I. (1985). Attachment theory: Retrospect and prospect. *Monographs of the Society for Research in Child Development, 50,* 3-35.

Briere, J. (1989). *Therapy for adults molested as children: Beyond survival.* New York: Springer.

Brockner, J., Derr, W. R., & Laing, W. N. (1987). Self-esteem and reaction to negative feedback: Toward greater generalizability. *Journal of Research in Personality, 21,* 318-333.

Brody, L.R., & Hall, J.A. (1993). Gender and emotion. In M. Lewis & J.M. Haviland (Eds.), *Handbook of emotions,* (pp. 447-460).

Brothers, L. (1990). The neural basis of primate social communication. *Motivation and Emotion, 14,* 81-91.

Buck, R. (1989). Emotional communication in personal relationships: A developmental-interactionist view. In C. Hendrick (Ed.), *Review of personality and social psychology: Vol. 10. Close relationships,* (pp. 144-163). Newbury Park, CA: Sage.

Buck, R., & Ginsburg B. (1997). Communicative genes and the evolution of empathy. In W. Ickes (Ed.). *Empathic accuracy* (pp. 17-43). New York: Guilford Press.

Burke, P. J. (1980). The self: Measurement requirements for an interactionist perspective. *Social Psychology Quarterly, 43,* 217-230.

Burns, D. D. (1980). *Feeling Good.* New York, NY: New American Library.

Bushman, B. J. & Baumeister, R. F. (1998). Threatened egotism, narcissism, self-esteem, and direct and displaced aggression: Does self-love or self-hate lead to violence? *Journal of Personality and Social Psychology, 75,* 219-229.

Byrne, R. W. (1995). The ape legacy: The evolution of Machiavellian intelligence and anticipatory interactive planning. In E. N. Goody (Ed.), *Social intelligence and interaction* (pp. 37-52). Cambridge: Cambridge University Press.

Caballo, V. E. (Ed.). (1998). *International handbook of cognitive and behavioural treatments for psychological disorders.* Kidlington, Oxford, England: Elsevier Science.

Campbell, J. D. (1990). Self-esteem and clarity of the self-concept. *Journal of Personality and Social Psychology, 59,* 538-549.

Campbell, J. D., Chew, B., & Scratchley, L. S. (1991). Cognitive and emotional reactions to daily events: The effects of self-esteem and self-complexity. *Journal of Personality, 59,* 473-505.

Campbell, J. D., & Lavallee, L. F. (1993). Who am I? The role of self-concept confusion in understanding the behavior of people with low self-esteem. In R.F. Baumeister (Ed.), *Self-esteem: The puzzle of low self-regard* (pp. 3-20). New York:Plenum Press.

Campbell, J. D., & Tesser, A. (1985). Self-evaluation maintenance processes in relationships. In S. Duck & D. Perlman (Eds.), *Understanding personal relationships: An interdisciplinary approach* (Vol. 1) (pp. 107-135). London: Sage Publications.

Campbell, J. M., & McCord, D. M. (1996). The WAIS-R Comprehension and Picture Arrangement subtests as measures of social intelligence: Testing traditional interpretations. *Journal of Psychoeducational Assessment, 14,* 240-249.

Carich, M.S., Henderson-Odum, N.V., & Metzger, C. (2001). *Enhancing victim empathy: A treatment context and selected victim empathy techniques.* Poster presentation at the Annual Research and Treatment Conference of the Association for the Treatment of Sexual Abusers, October, San Antonio, Texas.

Carkhuff, R.R. (1969). *Helping and human relations. Vol.2. Practice and Research.* New York: Holt, Rinehart & Winston.

Carkhuff, R.R., & Berenson, B.G. (1967). *Beyond counseling and therapy.* New York: Holt, Rinehart, & Winston.

Carkhuff, R.R., & Griffin, A.H. (1971). The selection and training of human relations specialists. *Journal of Counseling Psychology, 17,* 443-450.

Carkhuff, R.R., Kratochivil, D., & Friel, T. (1968). Effecs of professional training: Communication and discrimination of facilitative conditions. *Journal of Counseling Psychology, 15,* 68-74.

Carkhuff, R.R., & Pierce, R.M. (1975). *Trainer's guide: The act of helping.* Amherst, MA: Human Resource Development Press.

Cautela, J.R. (1996). Training the client to be empathetic. In J.R. Cautela & W. Ishaq (Eds.). Contemporary issues in behaviour therapy: Improving the human condition. *Applied Clinical Psychology* (pp. 337-353). New York, NY: Plenum Press.

Chapin, F. S. (1939). *The Social Insight Test.* Palo Alto, CA: Consulting Psychologists Press.

Chapin, F.S. (1942). Preliminary standardization of a social insight scale. *American Sociological Review, 7,* 214-225.

Chlopan, B.E., McCain, M.L., Carbonell, J.L., & Hagen, R.L. (1985). Empathy: Review of available measures. *Journal of Personality and Social Psychology, 44,* 113-126.

Clarizio, H. (1987). Differentiating emotional impaired from socially maladjusted students. *Psychology in the Schools, 24,* 237-243.

Clark, L.A., & Watson, D. (1991). General affective dispositions in physical and psychological health. In C.R. Snyder & D.R. Forsyth (Eds.), *Handbook of social and clinical psychology* (pp. 221-245). New York: Pergamon Press.

Cline, V. B., & Richards, J. M. (1960). Accuracy of interpersonal perception – a general trait? *Journal of Abnormal and Social Psychology, 60,* 1-70.

Cloitre, M. (1998). Sexual revictimization: Risk factors and prevention. In V. M. Follette, J. I. Ruzek & F. R. Abueg (Eds.), *Cognitive-behavioral therapies for trauma* (pp. 278-302). New York: Guilford Press.

Clore, G.L., Schwartz, N., & Conway, M. (1994). Affective causes and consequences of social information processing. In R.S. Wyer & T.K. Srull (Eds.), *Handbook of social cognition* (Vol. 1., pp. 323-417). Hillsdale, NJ: Erlbaum.

Coke, J.S., Batson, C.D., & McDavis, K. (1978). Empathic mediation of helping: A two-stage model. *Journal of Personality and Social Psychology, 36,* 752-766.

Colvin, C.R., Voigt, D., & Ickes, W. (1997). Why do friends understand each other better than strangers do? In W. Ickes (Ed.). *Empathic accuracy* (pp. 169-193). New York: Guilford Press.

Cooley, C.H. (1902). *Human nature and the social order.* New York: Charles Scribner's Sons.

Copleston, F. (1985). *A history of philosophy (Vol. I): Greece and Rome.* New York: Doubleday Books.

Cossio, S. G., Hernandez-Guzman, L., & Lopez, F. (2000). Are teacher ratings and peer nominations valid measures of social competence? *Revista Mexicana de Psicologia, 17,* 171-179.

Costa, P.T., & McCrae, R.R. (1988). Personality in adulthood: A six-year longitudinal study of self-ratings and spouse ratings on the NEO Personality Inventory. *Journal of Personality and Social Psychology, 54,* 853-863.

Cottrell, L.S. (1942). The analysis of situational fields in social psychology. *American Sociological Review, 7,* 374.

Cottrell, L.S., & Dymond, E. (1949). The empathy process. *Psychiatry, 12,* 355-359.

Cowen, E. L., Wyman, P. A., Work, W., & Parker, G. M. (1990). The Rochester child resilience study: Overview and summary of first year findings. *Development and Psychopathology, 2,* 193-212.

Crabb, W.T., Moracco, J.C., & Bender, R.C. (1983). A comparative study of empathy training with programmed instruction for lay helpers. *Journal of Counseling Psychology, 30,* 221-226.

Crandall, J.E. (1980). Adler's concept of social interest: Theory, measurement, and implications for adjustment. *Journal of Personality and Social Psychology, 39,* 481-495.

Cross, D.G., & Sharpley, C.F. (1982). Measurement of empathy with the Hogan Empathy Scale. *Psychological Reports, 50,* 62.

Dalton, R.F., Sunblad, L.M., & Hylbert, K.W. (1973). An application of principles of social learning to training in communication of empathy. *Journal of Counseling Psychology 20,* 378-383.

D'Antonio, A. (1997). *The effect of empathy on aggression and antisocial behaviour among low-impulsive and high-impulsive children and adolescents.* Dissertation Abstracts International: Section B: The Sciences & Engineering. 57, 7721.

Darwin, C. R. (1873). *The expression of the emotions in man and animals.* London: John Murray.

Davis, M. H. (1983). Empathic concern and the Muscular Dystrophy Telethon: Empathy as a multidimensional construct. *Personality and Social Psychology Bulletin, 9,* 223-229.

Davis, M.H. (1983). Measuring individual differences in empathy: Evidence for a multidimensional approach. *Journal of Personality and Social Psychology, 44,* 113-126.

Davis, M. H., & Franzoi, S. (1991). Stability and change in adolescent self-consciousness and empathy. *Journal of Research in Personality, 25,* 70-87.

Davis, M.H., & Kraus, L.A. (1997). Personality and empathic accuracy. In W. Ickes (Ed.). *Empathic accuracy* (pp. 144-168). New York: Guilford Press.

Deitz, S.R., Blackwell, K.T., Daley, P.C., & Bentley, B.J. (1982). Measurement of empathy toward rape victims and rapists. *Journal of Personality and Social Psychology, 43,* 372-384.

Deitz, S.R., Littman, M., & Bentley, B.J.(1984). Attribution of responsibility for rape: The influence of observer empathy, victim resistance, and victim attractiveness. *Sex Roles, 10,* 261-280.

Deutsch, F., & Madle, R.A. (1975). Empathy: Historic and current conceptualizations, and a cognitive theoretical perspective. *Human Development*, 18, 267-287.

Dodge, K. A. (1980). Social cognition and children's aggressive behavior. *Child Development*, 53, 620-635.

Dodgson, P. G., & Wood, J. V. (1998). Self-esteem and the cognitive accessibility of strengths and weaknesses after failure. Journal of Personality and Social Psychology, 75, 178-197.

Dryden, W. (1987). *Counselling individuals: The rational-emotive approach*. London: Taylor and Francis.

Dubow, E. F., & Tisak, J. T. (1989). The relation between stressful life events and adjustment in elementary school children: The role of social support and social problem-solving skills. *Child Development*, 60, 1412-1423.

Dunn, J., Bretherton, I., & Munn, P. (1987). Conversations about feeling states between mothers and their young children. *Developmental Psychology*, 23, 132-139.

Durant, W. (1961). *The story of philosophy: The lives and opinions of the great philosophers of the Western World*. New York: Simon and Schuster.

Dymond, R.F. (1949). A scale for the measurement of empathic ability. *Journal of Consulting Psychology*, 13, 127-133.

Dymond, R.F. (1950). Personality and empathy. *Journal of Consulting Psychology*, 14, 343-350.

Egan, G. (1975). *The skilled helper: A model for systematic helping and interpersonal relating*. Montery, CA: Brooks/Cole, 1975.

Eisenberg, N. (1986). *Altruistic cognition, emotion, and behavior*. Hillsdale, NJ: Lawrence Erlbaum.

Eisenberg, N. (2000). Empathy and sympathy. In M. Lewis & J.M. Haviland-Jones (Eds.). *Handbook of emotions* (2nd ed.) (pp.677-692) New York: Guilford Press.

Eisenberg, N., Carlo, G., Murphy, B., & Van Court, P. (1995). Prosocial development in late adolescence: A longitudinal study. *Child Development*, 66, 911-936.

Eisenberg, N., & Fabes, R.A. (1990). Empathy: Conceptualization, measurement, and relation to prosocial behvior. *Motivation and Emotion, 14,* 131-149.

Eisenberg, N., & Fabes, R.A. (1992). Emotion, regulation, and the development of social competence. In M.S. Clark (Ed.), *Review of personality and social psychology: Vol. 14. Emotion and social behavior* (pp. 119-150). Newbury Park, CA: Sage.

Eisenberg, N., Fabes, R. A., Schaller, M., & Miller, P. A. (1990). Sympathy and personal distress: Development, gender differences, and interrelations of indexes. In N. Eisenberg (Ed.) *Empathy and Related Emotional Responses,* (pp 107-126). San Francisco: Jossey-Bass.

Eisenberg, N., Guthrie. I. K., Cumberland, A., Murphy, B. C., Shepard, S. A., Zhou, Q., & Carlo, G. (2002). Prosocial development in early adulthood: A longitudinal study. *Journal of Personality and Social Psychology, 82,* 993-1006.

Eisenberg, N., McCreath, H., & Ahn, R. (1988). Vicarious emotional responsiveness and prosocial behavior: Their interrelations in young children. *Personality and Social Psychology Bulletin, 14,* 298-311.

Eisenberg, N., & Miller, P. (1987). The relation of empathy to prosocial and related behaviors. *Psychological Bulletin, 101,* 91-119.

Eisenberg, N., Murphy, B.C., & Shepard, S. (1997). The development of empathic accuracy. In W. Ickes (Ed.). *Empathic accuracy* (pp. 73-116). New York: Guilford Press.

Eisenberg, N., Shea, C.L., Carlo, G., & Knight, G. (1991). Empathy-related responding and cognition: A "chicken and the egg" dilemma. In W. Kurtines & J. Gerwitz (Eds.). *Handbook of moral behavior and development* (Vol 2.) (pp. 63-88). Hillsdale, N.J.: Lawrence Erlbaum.

Eisenberg, N., Shell, R., Pasternack, J., & Lennon, R. (1987). Prosocial development in middle childhood: A longitudinal study. *Developmental Psychology, 23,* 712-718.

Eisenberg, N., & Strayer, J. (1987). Critical issues in the study of empathy. In N. Eisenberg and J. Strayer (Eds.), *Empathy and its Development.* (pp. 47-80). New York: Cambridge University Press.

Eisenberg, N., & Strayer, J. (Eds.) (1987). *Empathy and its development.* Cambridge: Cambridge University Press.

Ekman, P. (1993). Facial expressions and emotion. *American Psychologist, 48,* 384-392.

Ekman, P., & Friesen, W.V. (1975). *Unmasking the face: A guide to recognizing emotions from facial clues.* Englewood Cliffs, NJ: Prentice-Hall.

Ekman, P., Friesen, W.V., & Ellsworth, P. (1972). *Emotion in the human face: Guidelines for research and an integration of findings.* New York: Pergamon Press.

Ekman, P., Levenson, R.W., & Friesen, W.V. (1983). Autonomic nervous system activity distinguishes among emotions. *Science, 221,* 1208-1210.

Ekman, P., & O'Sullivan, M. (1991). Facial expression: Methods, means, and moues. In R.S. Feldman & B. Rime (Eds.), *Fundamentals of nonverbal behavior* (pp. 163-199). Cambridge, UK: Cambridge University Press.

Engram, B.E., & Vandergoot, D. (1978). Correlation between the Truax and Carkhuff scales for measurement of empathy. *Journal of Counseling Psychology, 25,* 349-351.

Eysenck, H.J., & Eysenck, M.W. (1985). *Personality and individual differences: A natural science approach.* New York: Plenum Press.

Eysenck, S.B.F., & Eysenck, J.J. (1978). Impulsiveness and venturesomeness: Their position in a dimensional system of personality description. *Psychological Reports, 43,* 1247-1255.

Eysenck, S.B.G., & McGurk, B.J. (1980). Impulsiveness and venturesomeness in detention center population. *Psychological Reports, 47,* 1299-1306.

Felson, R. B. (2000). A social psychological approach to interpersonal aggression. In V. B. Van Hasselt & M. Hersen (Eds.), *Aggression and violence: An introductory text* (pp. 9-22). Boston: Allyn and Bacon.

Fernandez, Y. (2001, September). *Empathy issues in the treatment of sexual offenders: Client empathy and therapist empathy.* Plenary paper presented at the National Organization for the Treatment of Abusers Annual conference, Pontyprid, Wales, UK.

Fernandez, Y. M., Anderson, D. & Marshall, W. L. (1999). The relationship among empathy, cognitive distortions and self-esteem in sexual offenders. In Barbara K. Schwartz (Ed.) *The Sex Offender, Volume 3*. Kingston, NJ: Civic Research Institute.

Fernandez, Y.M., & Marshall, W.L. (in press). Violence, empathy, social self-esteem and psychopathy in rapists. *Sexual Abuse: A Journal of Research and Treatment*.

Fernandez, Y. M., Marshall, W. L., Lightbody, S., & O'Sullivan, C. (1999). The Child Molester Empathy Measure: Description and an examination of its reliability and validity. *Sexual Abuse: A Journal of Research and Treatment*, 11, 17-31.

Fernandez, Y.M., Marshall, W.L., Serran, G., Anderson, D., Marshall, L.E., & Mann, R.E. (2002) *Therapeutic process in sexual offender treatment: A manual prepared for the National Sex Offender Treatment Program - Moderate Intensity*. Unpublished manuscript.

Feshbach, N. D. (1969). Sex differences in children's modes of aggressive responses towards outsiders. *Merrill-Palmer Quarterly*, 15, 249-258.

Feshbach, S. (1970). Aggression. In P. H. Mussen (Ed.), *Carmichael's manual of child psychology*, (Vol. 2, pp. 159-259). New York: Wiley.

Feshbach, N.D. (1975). Empathy in children: Some theoretical and empirical considerations. *The Counseling Psychologist*, 5, 25-30.

Fesbach, N.D. (1978). Studies of empathic behavior in children. In B.A. Maher (Ed.). *Progress in personality research* (Vol. 8) (pp. 1-47). New York: Academic Press.

Feshbach, N. D. (1987). Parental empathy and child adjustment/ maladjustment. In N. Eisenberg & J. Strayer (Eds.), *Empathy and its development* (pp. 292-316). Cambridge: Cambridge University Press.

Feshbach, N. D. (1989). Empathy training and prosocial behavior. In J. Groebel & R. A. Hinde (Eds.), *Aggression and war: Their biological and social bases* (pp. 101-111). Cambridge: Cambridge University Press.

Feshbach, N. D., & Feshbach, S. (1969). The relationship between empathy and aggression in two age groups. *Developmental Psychology*, 1, 102-107.

Feshbach, N.D., & Roe, K. (1968). Learning to care: A positive approach to child training and discipline. *Journal of Clinical and Child Psychology*, 12, 266-271.

Festinger, L. (1957). *A theory of cognitive dissonance*. Evanston, IL: Row Peterson.

Ford, M. E. (1982). Social cognition and social competence in adolescence. *Developmental Psychology, 18*, 323-340.

Ford, M. E., & Tisak, M. S. (1983). A further search for social intelligence. *Journal of Educational Psychology, 75*, 196-206.

Fow, N.R. (1998). Partner-focused reversal in couple therapy. *Psychotherapy: Theory, Research, Practice, Training, 35*, 231-237.

Fox, N.A. (1995). Of the way we were: Adult memories about attachment experiences and their role in determining infant-parent relationships: A commentary on van Ijzendoorn (1995). *Psychological Bulletin, 117*, 404-410.

Frank, H., & Hoffman, N. (1986). Borderline empathy: An empirical investigation. *Comprehensive Psychiatry, 27*, 387-395.

Frederiksen, L. W., & Rainwater, N. (1981). Explosive behaviour: A skill development approach to treatment. In R. B. Stuart (Ed.), *Violent behavior: Social learning approaches to prediction, management and treatment* (pp. 265-288). New York: Brunner/Mazel.

Freud, S. (1922). *Group psychology and the analysis of the ego*. London: International Psycho-analytic Press.

Frick, R.W. (1985). Communicating emotion: The role of prosodic features. *Psychological Bulletin, 97*, 412-429.

Froman, R.D., & Peloquin, S.M. (2000). Rethinking the use of the Hogan Empathy Scale: A critical psychometric analysis. *American Journal of Occupational Therapy, 55*, 566-572.

Fultz, J., Schaller, M., & Cialdini, R.B. (1988). Empathy, sadness, and distress: Three related but distinct vicarious affective responses to another's suffering. *Personality and Social Psychology Bulletin, 14*, 312-325.

Gagnon, R., Hunse, C., & Patrick, J. (1988). Fetal responses to vibratory acoustic stimulation: Influence of basal heart rate. *American Journal of Obstetrics and Gynecology, 159*, 835-839.

Galton, F. (1869). *Hereditary genius*. New York: D. Appleton.

Gardner, H. (1983). *Frames of mind: The theory of multiple intelligences*. New York: Basic Books.

Gendreau, P., Burke, D., & Grant, B.A. (1980). A second evaluation of
the Rideau inmate volunteer program. *Canadian Journal of
Criminology, 22*, 66-77.

Gibbs, J. G., & Woll, S. B. (1985). Mechanisms used by young children in
the making of empathic judgements. *Journal of Personality, 53*, 575-585.

Gilbert, K.E., & Kuhn, H. (1939). *A history of esthetics*. New York:
MacMillan.

Ginsburg, B.E. (1991). Origins and dynamics of social organization in
primates and in wolves: Cooperation, aggression, and hierarchy. In
A. Somit & R. Wildemann (Eds.). *Hierarchy and democracy* (pp. 45-
62). Baden-Baden, Germany: Nomos.

Gladstein, A.G. (1983). Understanding empathy: Integrating counseling,
developmental and social psychology perspectives. *Journal of
Counseling Psychology, 30*, 467-482.

Gladstein, G.A. (1984). The historical roots of contemporary research.
Journal of the History of the Behavioral Sciences, 20, 38-59.

Glasser, A. J., & Zimmerman, I. L. (1967). *Clinical interpretation of the
Wechsler Intelligence Scale for Children*. New York: Grune & Stratton.

Goldberg, S. (1991). Recent developments in attachment theory and
research. *Canadian Journal of Psychiatry, 36*, 393-400.

Goldstone, J. (Producer), & Jones, T. (Director). (1983). Monty Python's
the meaning of life [Motion Picture]. United States: Celandine Films.

Goody, E.N. (1995). *Social intelligence and interaction*. Cambridge:
Cambridge University Press.

Gopnik, A., & Astington, J. W. (2000). Children's understanding of
representational change and its relation to the understanding of
false belief and the appearance-reality distinction. In K. Lee (Ed.)
Childhood Cognitive Development: the essential readings. (pp.177-200).
Malden, Mass, USA: Blackwell.

Gottshalk, R., Davidson, W. S., Mayer, J., & Gensheimer, L. K. (1987).
Behavioral approaches with juvenile offenders: A meta-analysis of
long-term treatment efficacy. In E. K. Morris & C. J. Braukmann
(Eds.), *Behavioral approaches to crime and delinquency: A handbook
of application, research, and concepts* (pp. 399-422). New York:
Plenum Press.

Gough, H.G. (1965). Conceptual analysis of psychological test scores and other diagnostic variables. *Journal of Abnormal Psychology, 70,* 294-302.

Greenberg, LS., & Goldman, R.L. (1988). *Journal of Clinical and Consulting Psychology, 56,* 696-702.

Greenberg, L.S., Rice, L.N., & Elliott, R. (1993). *Facilitating emotional change: The moment-by-moment process.* New York: Guilford Press.

Greenspan, S., Barenboim, C., & Chandler, M. J. (1976). Empathy and pseudo-empathy: The affective judgements of first- and third-graders. *Journal of Genetic Psychology, 129,* 77-88.

Greer, J. H., Estupinan, L. A., & Manguno-Mire, G. M. (2000). Empathy, social skills, and other relevant cognitive processes in rapists and child molesters. *Aggression and Violent Behavior, 5,* 99-126.

Guerrero, L.K. (1994). "I'm so mad I could scream": The effects of anger expression on relational satisfaction and communication competence. *The Southern Communication Journal, 59,* 125-141.

Guzetta, R.A. (1976). Acquisition and transfer of empathy by the parents of early adolescents through structured learning training. *Journal of Counseling Psychology, 23,* 449-453.

Hall, W.B. (1965). The empathy test. Reviewed in O.K. Buros, Jr. (Ed.), *Sixth mental measurements yearbook* (pp. 214-215). Highland Park, NJ: Gryphon Press.

Hamilton, W. D. (1964). The genetical evolution of social behavior. *Journal of Theoretical Biology, 7,* 1-52.

Hansen, J., Moore, G., & Carkhuff, R. (1968). The differential relationships of objective and client perceptions of counseling. *Journal of Clinical Psychology, 24,* 244-246.

Hanson, R.K. (in press). Assessing sexual offenders' capacity for empathy. *Psychology, Crime and Law.*

Hanson, R.K. (1997). Invoking sympathy – Assessment and treatment of empathy deficits among sexual offenders. In B.K. Schwartz & H.R. Cellini (Eds.). *The sex offender: New insights, treatment innovations and legal developments* (Vol. III) (pp. 1.1-1.12). Kingston, NJ: Civic Research Institute.

Hanson, R.K., & Scott, H. (1995). Assessing perspective-taking among sexual offenders, nonsexual criminals and nonoffenders. *Sexual Abuse: A Journal of Research and Treatment, 7,* 259-277.

Hayashino, D.S., Wurtele, S.K., & Klebe, K.J. (1995). Child molesters: An examination of cognitive factors. *Journal of Interpersonal Violence, 10,* 106-116.

Hennessy, M., Walter, J.S., & Vess, J. (2002). An evaluation of the Empat as a Measure of Victim Empathy with Civilly Committed Sexual Offenders. *Sexual Abuse: A Journal of Research and Treatment, 14,* 241-252.

Hickson, J. (1985). Psychological research on empathy: In search of an elusive phenomenon. *Psychological Reports, 57,* 91-94.

Higgens, W., Ivey, A., & Uhlemann, M. (1970). Media therapy: A programmed approach to teaching behavioural skills. *Journal of Counseling Psychology, 17,* 20-26.

Hildebran, D., & Pithers, W. D. (1989). Enhancing offender empathy for sexual abuse victims. In D. R. Laws (Ed.), *Relapse prevention with sex offenders* (pp. 236-243). New York: Guilford Press.

Hilton, Z. (1993). Childhood sexual victimization and lack of empathy in child molesters: Explanation or excuse? *International Journal of Offender Therapy and Comparative Criminology, 37,* 287-296.

Hodge, E.A., Payne, PA., & Wheeler, D.D. (1978). Approaches to empathy training: Programmed methods versus individual supervision and professional versus peer supervisors. *Journal of Counseling Psychology, 25,* 449-453.

Hodges, S.D., & Wegner, D.M. (1997). Automatic and controlled empathy. In W. Ickes (Ed). *Empathic accuracy* (pp. 311-339). New York: Guilford Press.

Hoffman, M. (1975). Developmental synthesis of affect and cognition and its implications for altruistic motivation. *Developmental Psychology, 11,* 607-622.

Hoffman, M. (1977). Sex differences in empathy and related behaviors. *Psychological Bulletin, 84,* 712-722.

Hoffman, M. (1981). Is altruism part of human nature? *Journal of Personality and Social Psychology, 40,* 121-137.

Hoffman, M. (1987). The contribution of empathy to justice and moral development. In N. Eisenberg and J. Strayer (Eds.), *Empathy and its Development*. (pp. 47-80). New York: Cambridge University Press.

Hoffman, M. (1990). Empathy and justice motivation. *Motivation and Emotion, 14,* 151-172.

Hogan, R. (1969). Development of an empathy scale. *Journal of Consulting and Clinical Psychology, 33,* 307-316.

Hogan, R., & Mankin, D. (1970). Determinants of interpersonal attraction: A clarification. *Psychological Reports, 35,* 58-63.

Hoppe, C.M., & Singer, R.D. (1976). Overcontrolled hositility, empathy, and egocentric balance in violent and nonviolent psychiatric offenders. *Psychological Reports, 39,* 405-445.

Hudson, S.M., Marshall, W.L., Wales, D., McDonald, E., Bakker, L.W., & McLean, A. (1993). Emotional recognition skills of sex offenders. *Annals of Sex Research, 6,* 199-211.

Huesmann, L. R. (1988). An information processing model for the development of aggression. *Aggressive Behavior, 14,* 13-24.

Hume, D. (1739). *A treatise of human nature.* Oxford: Clarendon Press.

Hunsdahl, J.B. (1967). Concerning einfuhlung (empathy): A concept analysis of its origin and early development. *Journal of the History of the Behavioral Sciences, 3,* 180-191.

Humphrey, N. K. (1976). The social function of intellect. In P. P. G. Bateson & R. A. Hinde (Eds.), *Growing points in ethology* (pp. 56-72). Cambridge: Cambridge University Press.

Hunt, T. (1927). What social intelligence is and where to find it. *Industrial Psychology, 2,* 605-612.

Hunt, T. (1928). The measurement of social intelligence. *Journal of Applied Psychology, 12,* 317-334.

Ickes, W. (1997) (Ed.) *Empathic accuracy.* New York: Guilford Press.

Ivey, A.E. (1971). *Microscounseling: Innovations in interviewing training.* Springfield, Il: Charles C. Thomas.

Ivey, A.E. (1973). Microcounseling: the counsellor as trainer. *Personnel and Guidance Journal, 51,* 311-316.

Izard, C.E. (1992). Basic emotions, relations among emotions, and emotion-cognition relations. *Psychological Review, 99,* 561-564.

Janis, I. L., & Mann, L. (1977). *Decision making: A psychological analysis of conflict, choice, and commitment.* New York, NY: The Free Press.

Johnson, J.A., Cheek, J.M., & Struther, R. (1983). The structure of empathy. *Journal of Personality and Social Psychology, 45,* 1299-1312.

Kagan, N., Krathwohl, D., Goldberg, A.D., Campbell, R.J., Schauble, P.G., Greenberg, B.S., Danish, S.J., Resnikoff, A., Bowes, J., & Bondy, S.B. (1967). *Studies in human interaction: Interpersonal process recall simulated by videotape.* East Lansing: Education Public Services.

Kalliopuska, M., & Tiitinen, U. (1991). Influence of two developmental programmes on the empathy and prosociability of preschool children. *Perceptual and Motor Skills, 72,* 323-328.

Karmiloff-Smith, A. (1996). The Connectionist Infant: Would Piaget Turn in his Grave? *SRCD Newsletter* (Fall issue), 1-10.

Katz, B. (1962). *Predictive and behavioral empathy and client change in short-term counseling.* Unpublished doctoral dissertation, New York University.

Katz, R.L. (1963). *Empathy: Its nature and uses.* London: Collier-Macmillan.

Kaukiainen, A., Bjorkqvist, K., Lagerspetz, K. M. J., Osterman, K., Salmivalli, C., Rothberg, S., & Ahlbom, A. (1999). The relationship between social intelligence, empathy, and different types of aggression. *Aggressive Behavior, 25,* 81-89.

Kaukiainen, A., Bjorkqvist, K., Osterman, K., & Lagerspetz, K. M. J. (1996). Social intelligence and empathy as antecedents of different types of aggression. In C. F. Ferris & T. Grisson (Eds.), *Understanding aggressive behavior in children* (pp. 364-366). New York: New York Academy of Sciences.

Kaukiainen, A., Bjorkqvist, K., Osterman, K., Lagerspetz, K. M. J., & Forsblom, S. (1995). *Peer-Estimated Social Intelligence (PESI).* Turku, Finland: Department of Psychology, University of Turku.

Kaukiainen, A., Bjorkqvist, K., Osterman, K., Lagerspetz, K. M. J., & Niskanen, L. (1994). *Social intelligence and the use of indirect aggression.* Presented at the XIII Biennal Meeting of the International Society for the Study of Behavioural Development, June 28-July 2, Amsterdam.

Kazdin, A. E. (1980). Covert and overt rehearsal and elaboration during treatment in the development of assertive behaviour. *Behaviour Research and Therapy, 18,* 191-201.

Keating, D. (1978). A search for social intelligence. *Journal of Educational Psychology, 70,* 218-223.

Keijsers, G.P.J., Schapp, C.P., & Hoogduin, C.A.L. (2000). The impact of interpersonal patient and therapist behavior on outcome in cognitive-behavior therapy. *Behavior Modification, 24,* 264-297.

Kendall, P.C., & Wilcox, L.E. (1980). Cognitive behavioral treatment for impulsivity: Concrete versus conceptual training in non-self-controlled problem children. *Journal of Consulting and Clinical Psychology, 48,* 80-91.

Kennedy-Moore, E. (1999). *Mood attributions and mood regulation: Beliefs about why we feel the way we feel.* Manuscript submitted for publication.

Kennedy-Moore, E., & Watson, J.C. (1999). How and when does emotional expression help? *Review of General Psychology, 5(3),* 187-212.

Kennedy-Moore, E., & Watson, J.D. (1999). *Expressing emotion: Myths, realities, and therapeutic strategies.* New York, NY: Guilford Press.

Kernis, M. H. (1993). The roles of stability and level of self-esteem in psychological functioning. (In R. Baumeister (Ed.), *Self-Esteem: The puzzle of low self-regard* (pp. 167-182). New York: Plenum.

Kerr, W. A., & Speroff, B. J. (1947). *The Empathy Test.* Chicago: Psychometric Affiliates.

Kerr, W.A., & Speroff, B.G. (1954). Validation and evaluation of the empathy test. *Journal of General Psychology, 50,* 369-376.

Kestenbaum, R., Farber, E. A., & Sroufe, L. A. (1989). Individual differences in empathy among preschoolers: Relation to attachment history. *New Directions for Child Development, No 44,* 51-64.

Kiesler, D. J. (1983). The 1982 interpersonal circle: A taxonomy for complementarity in human transactions. *Psychological Review, 90,* 185-214.

Kimberlin, C., & Friesen, D. (1977). Effects of client ambivalence, trainee conceptual level, and empathy training condition on empathic responding. *Journal of Counseling Psychology, 24,* 354-358.

Kisilevsky, B. S., & Muir, D. W. (1991). Human fetal and subsequent newborn responses to sound and vibration. *Infant Behavior and Development, 14,* 1-26.

Kohut, H. (1959). Introspection, empathy, and psychoanalysis. *Journal of the American Psychoanalytic Association, 7,* 459-483.

Kohut, H. (1978). *The search for the self* (Vols 1 & 2). New York: International Universities Press.

Kohut, H. (1984). *How does analysis cure?* Chicago: University of Chicago Press.

Kohut, H. (1990). The role of empathy in psychoanalytic cure: In R. Langs (Ed.)., *Classics in psychoanalytic techniques* (rev. ed.) pp. 463-473. Northvale, NJ: Aronson.

Kowalski, R. M. (1999). Speaking the unspeakable: Self-disclosure and mental health. In R. M. Kowalski and M. R. Leary (Eds.), T*he social psychology of emotional and behavioral problems: Interfaces of social and clinical psychology* (pp. 225-247). Washington, DC: American Psychological Association.

Kremer, J.F., & Dietzen, L.L. (1991). Two approaches to teaching accurate empathy to undergraduates: Teacher intensive and self-directed. *Journal of College Student Development, 32,* 69-75.

Kupfer, D.J., Drew, F.L., Curtis, E.K., & Rubenstein, D.N. (1978). Personality style and empathy in medical students. *Journal of Medical Education, 53,* 507-509.

Kurtines, W., & Hogan, R. (1972). Sources of conformity in unsocialized college students. *Journal of Abnormal Psychology, 80,* 49-51.

Kurtz, R.R., & Grummon, D.L. (1972). Different approaches to the measurement of therapist empathy and their relationship to therapy outcomes. *Journal of Consulting and Clinical Psychology, 1,* 106-115.

Lagerspetz, K. M. J., Bjorkqvist, K., & Peltonen, T. (1988). Is indirect aggression typical of females? Gender differences in aggressiveness in 11-to 12-year old children. *Aggressive Behavior, 14,* 403-414.

Langevin, R., Writght, M.A., & Handy, L. (1988). Empathy, assertiveness, aggressiveness, and defensiveness among sex offenders. *Annals of Sex Research, 1,* 533-547.

Lazarus, A. (1968). Behavior therapy and marriage counseling. *Journal of the American Society of Psychosomatic Dentistry and Medicine, 15,* 49-56.

Lee, K. (Ed.). (2000). *Childhood Cognitive Development: the essential readings.* Malden, Mass, USA: Blackwell.

Lee, V., & Anstruthers-Thompson, C. (1912). *Beauty and ugliness: And other studies in psychological aesthetics.* New York: John Lane.

Lesh, T. V. (1970). Zen meditation and empathy development. *Journal of Humanistic Psychology, 10,* 39-74.

Letourneau, C. (1981). Empathy and stress: How they affect parental aggression. *Social Work, 26,* 383-389.

Levenson, R.W. & Ruef, A.N. (1992). Empathy: A physiological substrate. *Journal of Personality and Social Psychology, 63,* 234-246.

Levinson, S. C. (1995). Interactional biases in human thinking. In E. N. Goody (Ed.), *Social intelligence and interaction* (pp. 221-260). Cambridge: Cambridge University Press.

Lewis, J.M. (1988). Empathy training for beginning therapists. *Hillside Journal of Clinical Psychiatry, 6,* 250-258.

Lewis, M & Haviland-Jones, J.M. (Eds.), (2000). *Handbook of emotions, 2nd Ed.* New York, NY: Guilford Press.

Lindgren, H.C., & Robinson, J. (1953). An evaluation of Dymond's test of empathy and insight. *Journal of Consulting Psychology, 17,* 172-176.

Linehan, M. (1988). *Skills training manual for treating borderline personality disorder.* New York: Guilford Press.

Linville, P. W. (1985). Self-complexity and affective extremity: Don't put all of your eggs in one basket. *Social Cognition, 3,* 94-120.

Linville, P. W. (1987). Self-complexity as a cognitive buffer against stress-related illness and depression. *Journal of Personality and Social Psychology, 52,* 663-676.

Lipps, T. (1903). Grundlegung der aesthetek: 1. Liepzig: Voss.

Lipps, T. (1913). *Zur einfuhlung.* Leipzig: Englemann.

Lipton, D.N., McDonel, E.C., & McFall, R.M. (1987). Heterosocial perception in rapists. *Journal of Consulting and Clinical Psychology, 55,* 17-21.

Listowel, W.A. (1933). *A critical history of modern aesthetics.* London: George Allen and Unwin.

Litvak-Miller, W., McDougall, D., & Romney, D. M. (1997). The structure of empathy during middle childhood and its relationship to prosocial behavior. *Genetic, Social, and General Psychology Monographs, 123,* 303-324.

Loeber, R. (1990). Development and risk factors of juvenile antisocial behavior and delinquency. *Clinical Psychology review, 10,* 1-41.

Long, E.C.J., Angera, J.J., Carter, S.J., Nakamoto, M., & Kalso M. (1999). Understanding the one you love: A longitudinal assessment of an empathy training program for couples on romantic relationships. *Family Relations, 48,* 235-242.

Lopez, N. L., Bonenberger, J. L., & Schneider, H. G. (2001). Parental disciplinary history, current levels of empathy, and moral reasoning in young adults. *North American Journal of Psychology, 3,* 193-204.

Maccoby, E. E., & Jacklin, C. N. (1974). *The psychology of sex differences.* Stanford, CA: Stanford University Press.

Malatesta, C.Z., & Haviland, J.M. (1982). Learning display rules: The socialization of emotion expression in infancy. *Child Development, 53,* 991-1003.

Mann, R.E., & Fernandez, Y.M. (2001). *SOTP Rolling Programme: Treatment Manual.* Unpublished manuscript.

Mann, R. E., & Thorton, D. (1998). The evolution of a multisite sexual offender treatment program. In W. L. Marshall, Y. M. Fernandez, S. M. Hudson & T. Ward (Eds.), *Sourcebook of treatment programs for sexual offenders* (pp. 47-57). New York: Prentice-Hall.

Marangoni, C., Garcia, S., Ickes, W., & Teng, G. (1995). Empathic accuracy in a clinically relevant setting. *Journal of Personality and Social Psychology, 68,* 854-869.

Marlowe, H. A. (1986). Social intelligence: Evidence for multidimensionality and construct independence. *Journal of Educational Psychology, 78,* 52-58.

Marshall, W.L., Anderson, D., & Fernandez, Y.M. (1999). *Cognitive behavioural treatment of sexual offenders.* Chichester, England: John Wiley & Sons.

Marshall, W. L., & Barbaree, H. E. (1984). Disorders of personality, impulse and adjustment. In S. M. Turner & M. Hersen (Eds.), *Adult psychopathology: A behavioral perspective* (pp. 406-449). New York: John Wiley & Sons.

Marshall, W.L., Champagne, F., Brown, C., & Miller, S. (1997). Empathy, intimacy, loneliness, and self-esteem in nonfamilial child molesters. *Journal of Child Sexual Abuse, 6,* 87-97.

Marshall, W.L., Champagne, F., Sturgeon, C., & Bryce, P. (1997). Increasing the self-esteem of child molesters. *Sexual Abuse: A Journal of Research and Treatment, 9,* 321-333.

Marshall, W. L., & Fernandez, Y. M. (2001). Empathy training. In M. S. Carich & S. E. Mussack (Eds.), *Handbook for sexual abuser assessment and treatment* (pp. 141-147). Brandon, VT: Safer Society Press.

Marshall, W.L., Fernandez, Y.M., Serran, G.A., Mulloy, R., Thornton, D., Mann, R.E., & Anderson, D. (in press). Process variables in the treatment of sexual offenders: A review of the relevant literature. *Aggression and Violent Behavior: A Review Journal.*

Marshall, W.L., Hamilton, K., & Fernandez, Y.M. (1998). Empathy deficits and cognitive distortions in child molesters. *Sexual Abuse: A Journal of Research and Treatment, 13,* 123-131.

Marshall, W.L., Hudson, S.M., Jones, R., & Fernandez, Y.M. (1995). Empathy in sex offenders. *Clinical Psychology Review, 15,* 99-113.

Marshall, W.L., Jones, R., Hudson, S.M., & McDonald, E. (1993). Generalized empathy in child molesters. *Journal of Child Sexual Abuse, 2,* 61-68.

Marshall, W.L., & Maric A. (1996). Cognitive and emotional components of generalized empathy deficits in child molesters. *Journal of Child Sexual Abuse, 5,* 101-110.

Marshall, W.L., O'Sullivan, C., & Fernandez, Y.M. (1996). The enhancement of victim empathy among incarcerated child molesters. *Legal and Criminological Psychology, 1,* 95-102.

Marshall, W. L., & Serin, R. (1997). Personality disorders. In S. M. Turner & M. Hersen (Eds.), *Adult psychopathology and diagnosis (3rd ed.)* (pp. 508-543). New York: John Wiley & Sons.

Marshall, W. L., Serran, G., Moulden, H., Mulloy, R., Fernandez, Y. M., Mann, R. E. & Thornton, D. (in press). Therapist features in sexual offender treatment: Their reliable identification and influence on behavior change. *Clinical Psychology and Psychotherapy*.

Martin, G. B., & Clark, R. D., (1982). Distress crying in neonates: Species and peer specificity. *Developmental Psychology, 18*, 3-9.

Martin, G., & Pear, J. (1992). *Behavior modification: What it is and how to do it.* (4th ed.). Englewood Cliffs, N.J.: Prentice Hall.

Masten, A. S., Coatsworth, J. D., Neeman, J., Gest, S. D., Tellegan, A., & Garmezy, N. (1995). The structure and coherence of competence from childhood through adolescence. *Child Development, 66*, 1635-1639.

McCann, I.L., & Pearlman, L.A. (1990). *Psychological trauma and the adult survivor: Theory, therapy, and transformation.* New York: Brunner/Mazel.

McClatchy, V.R. (1929). A theoretical and statistical critique of the concept of social intelligence and attempts to measure such a process. *Journal of Abnormal and Social Psychology, 24*, 217-220.

McCown, W., Johnson, J., & Austin, S. (1986). Inability of delinquents to recognize facial affects. *Journal of Social Behavior and Personality, 1(4)*, 489-496.

McCrae, R.R. (1982). Consensual validation of personality traits: Evidence from self-reports and ratings. *Journal of Personality and Social Psychology, 43*, 293-303.

McDougall, W. (1908). *An introduction to social psychology.* Boston: Luce.

McFall, R.M. (1982). A review and reformulation of the concept of social skills. *Behavioral Assessment, 4*, 1-33.

McFarlin, D. B., & Blascovich, J. (1981). Effects of self-esteem and performance feedback on future affective preferences and cognitive expectations. *Journal of Personality and Social Psychology, 40*, 521-531.

McGrath, M., Cann, S., & Konopasky, R.J. (1998). New measures of defensiveness, empathy, and cognitive distortions for sexual offenders against children. *Sexual Abuse: A Journal of Research and Treatment, 10*, 25-36.

Mead, G.H. (1934). *Mind, self, and society.* Chicago: University of Chicago Press.

Mehrabian, A., & Epstein, N. (1972). A measure of emotional empathy. *Journal of Personality*, 40, 525-543.

Mergenthaler, E. (1996). Emotion-abstraction patterns in verbatim protocols: A new way of describing therapeutic processes. *Journal of Consulting and Clinical Psychology*, 64, 1306-1315.

Miller, P.A., & Eisenberg, N. (1988). The relation of empathy to aggressive and externalizing/antisocial behavior. *Psychological Bulletin*, 103, 324-344.

Miller, R.S., & Leary, M.R. (1992). Social sources and interactive functions of emotion: The case of embarrassment. In M.S. Clark (Ed.), *Review of Personality and Social Psychology* (Vol. 14, pp. 202-221). Newbury Park, CA: Sage.

Miller, W.R., Benefield, R.G., & Tonigan, J.S. (1993). Enhancing motivation for change in problem drinking: A controlled comparison to two therapist styles. *Journal of Consulting and Clinical Psychology*, 61, 455-461.

Miller, W. R., & Rollnick, S. (1991). *Motivational interviewing: Preparing people to change addictive behavior*. New York:Guilford Press.

Miller, W.R., & Sovereign, R.G. (1989). The check-up: A model for early intervention in addictive behaviors. In T. Loberg, W.R. Miller, P.E. Nathan, & G.A. Marlatt (Eds.), *Addictive behaviors: Prevention and early intervention* (pp. 219-231). Amsterdam: Swets & Zeitlinger.

Miller, W.R., Taylor, C.A., & West, J.C. (1980). Focused versus broad-spectrum behavior therapy for problem-drinkers. *Journal of Consulting and Clinical Psychology*, 48, 590-601.

Mischel, W. (1968). *Personality and assessment*. New York: John Wiley & Sons.

Mitchell, K.N., Rubin, S.E., Bozarth, J.D., & Wyrick, T.J. (1971). Effects of short-term training on residence hall assistants. *Counselor Education and Supervision*, 10, 310-318.

Moore, B. S. (1990). The origins and development of empathy. *Motivation and Emotion*, 14, 75-90.

Moreland, J.R., Ivey, A.E., & Phillips, J.S. (1973). An evaluations of microcounseling as an interviewer training tool. *Journal of Consulting and Clinical Psychology*, 41, 294-300.

Moreno, J. (1953). *Who shall survive?* New York: Beacon.

Moreno, J.(1946). *Psychodrama.* New York: Beacon.

Morris, E. K., & Braukmann, C. J. (Eds.). (1987). *Behavioral approaches to crime and delinquency: A handbook of application, research, and concepts.* New York: Plenum Press.

Moss, F. A., Hunt, T., Omwake, K. T., & Ronning, M. M. (1927). *Social intelligence test.* Washington, D. C.: Center for Psychological Service.

Moulden, H., & Marshall, W.L. (2002). *Assessing social intelligence and empathy in sexual offenders: Project in process.* Rockwood Psychological Services, Kingston, Ontario, Canada.

Mueser, K. T. (1998). Cognitive behavioural treatment of schizophrenia. In V. E. Caballo (Ed.), *International handbook of cognitive and behavioural treatments for psychological disorders* (pp. 551-570). Kidlington, Oxford, England: Elsevier Science.

Muir, D., & Slater, A. (Eds.). (2000). *Infant Development: The essential readings.* Malden, Mass, USA: Blackwell.

Murphy, W.D., Coleman, E.M., & Haynes, M.R. (1986). Factors related to coercive sexual behavior in a nonclinical sample of males. *Violence and Victims, 1,* 255-278.

Nicoletta, L.K. (2000). The effects of three training interventions on the development of resilient qualities in adolescent females. *Dissertation Abstracts International: Section B: The Sciences & Engineering. 61,* 1092.

Nolen-Hoeksema, S. (1987). Sex differences in unipolar depression: Evidence and theory. *Psychological Bulletin, 101,* 259-282.

Nunnally, J., & Bernstein, I. (1994). *Psychometric theory* (3rd ed.). New York: McGraw-Hill.

Ohbuchi, K. (1988). Arousal of empathy and aggression. *Psychologia: An International Journal of Psychology, 31,* 177-186.

Orotny, A., Clore, G.L., & Foss, M. (1987). The referential structure of the affective lexicon. *Cognitive Science, 11,* 361-384.

Papousek, M., Bornstein, M. H., Nuzzo, C., Papousek, H., & Symmes, D. (2000). Infant responses to prototypical melodic contours in parental speech. In D. Muir, & A. Slater (Eds.), *Infant Development: The essential readings.* (pp 261-281). Malden, MA, USA: Blackwell.

Patterson, G.R., & Forgatch, M.S. (1985). Therapist behavior as a determinant for client noncompliance: A paradox for the behavior modifier. *Journal of Consulting and Clinical Psychology, 53,* 846-851.

Paul, E. S. (2000). Empathy with animals and with humans: Are they linked? *Anthrozoos, 13,* 194-202.

Payne, P.A., Weiss, S.D., & Knapp, R.A. (1972). Didactic, experiential, and modeling factors in the learning of empathy. *Journal of Counseling Psychology, 19,* 425-429.

Pennebaker, J.W. (1995). *Emotion, disclosure, and health.* Washington, DC: American Psychological Association.

Perkins, S.R., & Atkinson, D.R. (1973). Effects of selected techniques for training resident assistants in human relations skills. *Journal of Counseling Psychology, 20,* 84-90.

Perls, F. (1969). *Gestalt therapy verbatim.* Lafayette: Real People.

Perry, M.A. (1975). Modeling and instructions in training for counselor empathy. *Journal of Counseling Psychology, 22,* 173-179.

Piaget, J. (1929). *The child's conception of the world.* New York: Harcourt Brace.

Piaget, J. (1932). *The moral judgement of the child.* London: Kegan Paul.

Pierce, R.M., & Drasgow, J. (1969). Teaching facilitative interpersonal functioning to psychiatric patients. *Journal of Counseling Psychology, 16,* 295-298.

Pithers, W.D. (1994). Process evaluation of a group therapy component designed to enhance sex offenders' empathy for sexual abuse survivors. *Behaviour Research and Therapy, 32,* 565-570.

Pithers, W.D. (1997). Maintaining treatment integrity with sexual abusers. *Criminal Justice and Behaviour, 24,* 34-51.

Pithers, W.D. (1999). Empathy: Definition, enhancement, and relevance to the treatment of sexual abusers. *Journal of Interpersonal Violence, 14,* 257-284.

Platt, J. J., & Prout, M. F. (1987). Cognitive-behavioral therapy and interventions for crime and delinquency. In E. K. Morris & C. J. Braukmann (Eds.), *Behavioral approaches to crime and delinquency: A handbook of application, research, and concepts* (pp. 477-497). New York: Plenum Press.

Plutchik, R. (1980). *Emotion: A psychoevolutionary synthesis.* New York: Harper and Row.

Plutchik, R. (1983). Emotions in early development: A psychoevolutionary approach. In R. Plutchik and H. Kellerman (Eds.), *Emotions in early development* (vol. 2). New York: Academic Press.

Plutchik, R. (1987). Evolutionary bases of empathy. In N. Eisenberg and J. Strayer (Eds.). *Empathy and Its Development* (pp. 38-63). New York: Cambridge University Press.

Premack, D. (1988). 'Does the chimpanzee have a theory of mind' revisited. In R. W. Byrne & A. Whiten (Eds.) *Machiavellian Intelligence: Social expertise and the evolution of intellect in monkeys, apes, and humans.* (pp. 160-179). New York: Clarendon Press/ Oxford University Press.

Rader, M.M. (1935). *A modern book of esthetics: An anthology.* New York: Holt.

Rapaport, K., & Burkhart, B.R. (1984). Personality and attitudinal characteristics of sexually coercive college males. *Journal of Abnormal Psychology, 93,* 216-221.

Rappaport, J., & Chinsky, J.M. (1972). Accurate empathy: Confusion of a construct. *Psychological Bulletin, 77,* 400-404.

Reik, T. (1948). *Listening with the third ear.* New York: Grove Press.

Rice, L.N. (1974). The evocative function of the therapist. In D. Wexler & L.N. Rice, (Eds.), *Innovations in client-centered therapy* (pp. 289-311). New York: Wiley.

Rice, L.N., & Saperia, E. (1984). A task analysis of the resolution of problematic reaction. In L.N. Rice & L.S. Greenberg (Eds.), *Patterns of change: Intensive analysis of psychotherapy process* (pp. 29-66). New York: Guilford Press.

Rice, M.E., Chaplin, T.E., Harris, G.E., & Coutts, J. (1990). *Empathy for the victim and sexual offender among rapists.* Penetanguishene Mental Health Centre, Research Report No.7.

Rice, M.E., Chaplin, T.E., Harris, G.E., & Coutts, J. (1994). Empathy for the victim and sexual arousal among rapists and nonrapists. *Journal of Interpersonal Violence, 9,* 435-449.

Richardson, R., Hammock, G. S., Smith, S. M., Gardner, W., & Signo, M. (1994). Empathy as a cognitive inhibitor of interpersonal aggression. *Aggressive Behavior, 20,* 275-289.

Robinson, J., Zahn-Waxler, C., & Emde, R. N. (2001). Relationship context as a moderator of sources of individual differences in empathic development. In R. N. Emde & J. K. Hewitt (Eds.), *Infancy to Early Childhood: Genetic and Environmental Influences on Developmental Change,* (pp 257-268). New York: Oxford University Press.

Rodin, J., Elias, M., Silberstein, L. R., & Wagner, A. (1988). Combined behavioral and pharmacologic treatment for obesity: Predictors of successful weight maintenance. *Journal of Consulting and Clinical Psychology, 56,* 399-404.

Roe, K. V. (1980). Toward a contingency hypothesis of empathy development. *Journal of Personality and Social Psychology, 39,* 991-994.

Rogers, C.R. (1942). *Counseling and psychotherapy.* Boston: Houghton Mifflin.

Rogers, C.R. (1951). *Client-centered therapy.* Boston: Houghton Mifflin.

Rogers, C.R. (1957). The necessary and sufficient conditions of therapeutic personality change. *Journal of Consulting Psychology, 21,* 95-103.

Rogers, C.R. (1959). A theory of therapy, personality, and interpersonal relationships as developed in the client-centered framework. In S. Koch (Ed.). *Psychology: The study of a science Vol. 3. Formulations of the person and the social context* (pp. 184-256). New York: McGraw-Hill.

Rogers, C.R. (1975). Empathic: An unappreciated way of being. *The Counseling Psychologist, 2,* 2-10.

Rogers, C.R., Gendlin, E.T., Kiesler, D.J., & Truax, C.B (Eds.) (1967). *The therapeutic relationship and its impact: A study of psychotherapy with schizophrenics.* Madison: University of Wisconsin Press.

Rosenberg, R. (1965). *Society and the adolescent self-image.* Princeton, NJ: Princeton University Press.

Rutter, M. (1990). Psychosocial resilience and protective mechanisms. In J. Rolf, A. S. Masten, D. Cicchetti, K. H. Nuechterlein & S. Weintraub (Eds.), *Risk and protective factors in the development of psychopathology* (pp. 181-214). New York: Cambridge University Press.

Safran, J.D. & Segal, Z.V. (1990). *Interpersonal process in cognitive therapy.* New York, NY: Basic Books, Inc.

Sagi, A., & Hoffman, M. L. (1976). Empathic distress in the newborn. *Developmental Psychology, 12,* 175-176.

Scheff, T. (1979). *Catharsis in healing, ritual, and drama.* Berkeley: University of California Press.

Scheler, M. (1913). *The nature of sympathy* (trans P. Heath). Hamden, CT: Shoestring Press.

Scherer, K.R., Wallbott, H.G., Matsumoto, D., & Kudoh, T. (1988). Emotional experience in cultural context: A comparison between Europe, Japan, and the United States. In K.R. Scherer (Ed.), *Facets of emotion: Recent research* (pp. 5-30). Hillsdale, NJ: Erlbaum.

Schwarz, N. (1990). Feelings as information: Informational and motivational functions of affective states. In E.T. Higgins & R.M. Sorrentino (Eds.), *Handbook of motivation and cognition: Foundations of social behavior* (Vol. 2, pp. 527-561). New York: Guilford Press.

Scully, D. (1988). Convicted rapists' perceptions of self and victim: Role taking and emotions. *Gender and Society, 2,* 200-213.

Serran, G.A., Fernandez, Y.M., Marshall, W.L., & Mann, R.E. (in press). Process issues in treatment: Applications to sexual offender programs. *Professional Psychology: Research and Practice.*

Seto, M.C. (1992). *Victim blame, empathy, and discrimination of sexual arousal to rape in community males and incarcerated rapists.* Unpublished M.A. Thesis, Queen's University, Kingston, Ontario, Canada.

Shafer, R. (1967). *Projective testing and psychoanalysis.* New York, NY: International Universities Press.

Shafer, W.F., & Hummel, T.J. (1979). Three experiments using an algorithm for empathic responses. *Journal of Counseling Psychology, 26,* 279-284.

Shaver, K.G. (1970). Defensive attribution: Effects of severity and relevance on the responsibility assigned for an accident. *Journal of Personality and Social Psychology, 14,* 101-113.

Shaver, P.R., Schwartz, J., Kirson, D., & O'Connor, C. (1987). Emotion knowledge: Further explorations of a prototypic approach. *Journal of Personality and Social Psychology, 52,* 1061-1086.

Shelton, (1969).

Shrauger, J. S. (1975). Responses to evaluation as a function of initial self-perceptions. *Psychological Bulletin, 82,* 581-596.

Shrauger, J. S., & Rosenberg, S. E. (1970). Self-esteem and the effects of success and failure feedback on performance. *Journal of Personality, 38,* 404-417.

Sillars, A.L., & Scott, M.D. (1983). Interpersonal perception between intimates: An integrative review. *Human Communications Research,* 10, 153-176.

Simpson, J. A. (1999). Attachment theory in modern evolutionary perspective. In J. Cassidy & P. R. Shaver (Eds.), *Handbook of Attachment: theory, research, and clinical applications.* pp. 115-140. New York: Guilford.

Slater, A. (2000). Visual perception in the young infant: Early organization and rapid learning. In D. Muir, & A. Slater (Eds.), *Infant Development: The essential readings.* (pp 95-116). Malden, MA, USA: Blackwell.

Smallbone, S. W., & Dadds, M. R. (2000). Attachment and coercive sexual behavior. *Sexual Abuse: Journal of Research & Treatment.* 12, 3-15.

Smith, A. (1759). *The theory of moral sentiments.* London: Strahan.

Spearman, C. E. (1927). *The abilities of man.* London: Macmillan.

Spencer, S. J., Josephs, R. A., & Steele, C. M. (1993). Low self-esteem: The uphill struggle for self-integrity. In R.F. Baumeister (Ed.), *Self-esteem: The puzzle of low self-regard* (pp. 21-36). New York: Plenum Press.

Sroufe, L. A., Egeland, B., & Kreutzer, T. (1990). The fate of early experience following developmental change: Longitudinal approaches to individual adaptation in childhood. *Child Development, 61,* 1363-1373.

Stearns, P.N. (1989). *Jealousy: The evolution of an emotion in American history.* New York: New York University Press.

Stermac, L.E., & Segal, Z.V. (1989). Adult sexual contact with children: An examination of cognitive factors. *Behavior Therapy, 20,* 573-584.

Sternberg, R. J., & Smith, C. (1985). Social intelligence and decoding skills in nonverbal communication. *Social Cognition, 3,* 168-192.

Stewart, D.A. (1956). *Preface to empathy.* New York: Philosophical Library.

Stone, G.L., & Vance, A. (1976). Implications for training. *Journal of Counseling Psychology, 23,* 272-279.

Stotland, E. (1969). Exploratory investigations of empathy. In L. Berkowitz (Ed.). *Advances in experimental social psychology* (Vol. 4) (pp. 271-314). New York: Academic Press.

Strayer, J. (1993). Children's concordant emotions and cognitions in response to observed emotions. *Child Development, 64,* 188-201.

Strayer, J., & Roberts, W. (1997). Children's personal distance and their empathy: indices of interpersonal closeness. *International Journal of Behavioral Development, 20,* 385-403.

Streit-Forest, U. (1982). Differences in empathy: A preliminary analysis. *Journal of Medical Education, 57,* 65-67.

Sullivan, H.S. (1947). *Conceptions of modern psychiatry.* Washington, DC: White Foundation.

Symons, L. A., Hains, S. M., & Muir, D. W. (2000). Look at me: Five-month-old infants' sensitivity to very small deviations in eye-gaze during social interactions. In D. Muir, & A. Slater (Eds.), *Infant Development: The essential readings.* (pp 139-146). Malden, MA, USA: Blackwell.

Tangney, J. P. & Dearing, R. L. (2002). *Shame and guilt.* New York, NY: Guilford Press.

Taylor, S. E., & Brown, J. D. (1988). Illusion and well-being: A social psychological perspective on mental health. *Psychological Bulletin, 103,* 193-210.

Thelen, E. (1995). Motor development: A new synthesis. *American Psychologist. 50,* 79-95.

Thomas, G., & Fletcher, G.J.O. (1997). Empathic accuracy in close relationships. In W. Ickes (Ed.). *Empathic accuracy* (pp. 194-217). New York: Guilford Press.

Thomson, R. A. (1987). Empathy and emotional understanding. In N. Eisenberg and J. Strayer (Eds.), *Empathy and its Development,* (pp. 119-145). New York: Cambridge University Press.

Thorndike, E. L. (1920). Intelligence and is use. *Harper's Magazine,* 140, 227-235.

Thorndike, E.L. (1959). The empathy test. Review of O.K. Buros, Jr. (Ed.), In *The fifth mental measurement yearbook* (pp. 120-121).

Thurstone, L. L. (1938). *Primary mental abilities.* Chicago: University of Chicago Press.

Tice, D. M. (1993). The social motivations of people with low self-esteem. In R.F. Baumeister (Ed.), *Self-esteem: The puzzle of low self-regard* (pp. 37-53). New York: Plenum Press.

Titchener, E.B. (1909). *Lectures on the experimental psychology of the thought-processes.* New York: Macmillan.

Toi, M., & Batson, C.D. (1982). More evidence that empathy is a source of altruistic motivation. *Journal of Personality and Social Psychology,* 43, 281-292.

Toukmanian, S.G., & Rennie, D.L. (1975). *Journal of Counseling Psychology,* 22, 345-352.

Trommsdorff, G. (1991). Child-rearing and children's empathy. *Perceptual and Motor Skills,* 72, 387-390.

Truax, C.B. (1961). A scale for the measurement of accurate empathy. In *Wisconsin Psychiatric Institute Discussion Paper 20.* Madison, WI, Wisconsin Psychiatric Institute.

Truax, C.B. (1966). Therapist empathy, warmth, and genuineness and patient personality change in group psychotherapy: A comparison of unit measures, time, sample measures, patient perception measures. *Journal of Clinical Psychology,* 22, 225-229.

Truax, C.B., & Carkhuff, R.R. (1967). *Toward effective counseling and psychotherapy.* Chicago: Aldine.

Ungerer, J. A., Dolby, R., Waters, B., Barnett, B., Kelk, N., & Lewin, V. (1990). The early development of empathy: Self-regulation and individual differences in the first year. *Motivation and Emotion,* 14, 93-106.

Van Ornum, W., Foley, J.M., Burns, R., DeWolfe, A.S., & Kennedy, E.C. (1981). Empathy, altruism, and self-interest in college students. *Adolescence, 16*, 799-808.

Vernon, P.E. (1933). Some characteristics of the good judge of personality. *Journal of Social Psychology, 4*, 42-57.

Walden, R., & Ogan, T. (1988). The development of social referencing. *Child Development, 59*, 1230-1240.

Waldron, F.S. (1996). *Process variables: Four common elements of counseling and psychotherapy.* New York, NY: Brooks/Cole Publishing.

Walker, R. E., & Foley, J. M. (1973). Social intelligence: Its history and measurement. *Psychological Reports, 33*, 839-864.

Ward, T., Keenan, T, & Hudson, S. M. (2000). Understanding cognitive, affective, and intimacy deficits in sexual offenders: A developmental perspective. *Aggression and Violent Behavior, 5*, 41-62.

Watson, J.C., & Greenberg, L.S. (1996). Emotion and cognition in experiential therapy: A dialectical-constructivist position. In H. Rosen & K.T. Kuehlwein (Eds.), *Constructing realities: Meaning-making perspectives for psychotherapists* (pp. 253-274). San Francisco: Jossey-Bass.

Webster, S. D., Bowers, L. E., Mann, R. E., & Marshall, W. L. (2002). *Developing empathy in sex offenders: The value of offence re-enactments.* Submitted for publication.

Wechsler, D. (1958). *The measurement and appraisal of adult intelligence.* (4th ed.). Baltimore: Williams & Wilkins.

Wedeck, J. (1947). The relationship between personality and 'psychological ability.' *British Journal of Psychology, 37*, 133-151.

Weinstein, E. A. (1969). The development of interpersonal competence. In D. A. Goslin (Ed.), *Handbook of socialization theory and research* (pp. 753-775). Chicago: Rand McNally.

Wells, L. E., & Marwell, G. (1976). *Self-esteem.* Beverly Hills, CA: Sage Publications.

Werner, E. E., & Smith, R.S. (1992). *Overcoming the odds: High-risk children from birth to adulthood.* Ithaca, NY: Cornell University Press.

Williams, C.A. (1990). Biopsychosocial elements of empathy: A multidimensional model. *Issues in Mental Health Nursing, 11*, 155-174.

Wills, T. A. (1981). Downward comparison principles in social psychology. *Psychological Bulletin, 90,* 245-271.

Wind, E. (1963). *Art and anarchy.* London: Faber & Faber.

WispÈ, L. (1986). The distinction between sympathy and empathy: To call forth a concept, a word is needed. *Journal of Personality and Social Psychology, 50,* 314-321.

Zahn-Waxler, C., Robinson, J. L., & Emde, R. N. (1992). The development of empathy in twins. *Developmental Psychology, 28,* 1038-1047.

Zhan-Waxler, C., Schiro, K., Robinson, J. L., Emde, R. N., & Schmitz (2001). Empathy and prosocial patterns in young MZ and DZ twins: Development and genetic and environmental influences. In R. N. Emde & J. K. Hewitt (Eds.) *Infancy to Early Childhood: Genetic and Environmental Influences on Developmental Change* (pp. 141-162). New York: Oxford University Press.

Zucker, P.J., Worthington, E.L., & Forsyth, D.R. (1985). Increasing empathy through participation in structured groups: Some attritbutional evidence. *Human Relations, 38,* 247-255.

Zuckerman, M. (1995). Good and bad humors: Biochemical bases of personality and its disorders. *Psychological Science, 6,* 325-332.

CONTRIBUTORS

Yolanda Fernandez, Ph.D. graduated with a BA (H) in 1994, an M.A. in 1996, and a Ph.D. in Clinical/ Forensic Psychology in 2001 from Queen's University in Kingston, Ontario, Canada. She is currently the Clinical Director of Rockwood Psychological Services, and the Clinical Director of the Sexual Offender Treatment Program at Bath Institution (a medium-security federal penitentiary). Yolanda has also provided training workshops on Effective Therapist Characteristics in Working with Sexual Offenders in several different countries. In addition to her clinical work Yolanda is an active researcher who currently has several presentations at international conferences and over 20 publications. Her publications include one co-authored book, one edited, and one co-edited book. Yolanda's research interests include therapeutic process in sexual offender treatment, empathy deficits in sexual offenders, and phallometric testing with sexual offenders. She is presently acting as the Student Representative and is chair of the Student Committee for the Association for the Treatment of Sexual Abusers (ATSA).

Dana Anderson, Ph.D., is the Clinical Director of the Tupiq Program for Inuit Offenders at Fenbrook Institution, a medium-security federal penitentiary in Canada, and has previously served as the Clinical Director for the Sexual Offender Treatment Program at Kingston Penitentiary, a maximum-security institution. She is an active researcher whose publications include one co-authored book on the treatment of sexual offenders. Her research interests include treatment modalities, personality, substance abuse, and aboriginal offenders.

Maxine Daniels originally trained as a drama teacher. She has combined psychology and drama to use role-play as a therapeutic tool in treatment with offenders. She has just completed her training as a psychodramatist/psychotherapist. Maxine is role-play consultant to Her Majesty's Prison Service (England) and works with the Sex Offender Treatment Programme (SOTP), Adapted SOTP, CSCP, (violent offenders) and Focus (Drugs Programme). She has trained facilitators in Scotland, Ireland, Finland, Wisconsin, USA and secure hospitals in England. She works in private practice as a psychodramatist/ psychotherapist. Maxine is also a director of Creative Forum a company that specialises in interactive role-play training that works in corporate businesses, health service and education.

Philip Dodgson, Ph.D. is Associate Director of Assessment Services at the Southdown Institute, a residential treatment centre specializing in the treatment of clergy and religious professionals. His clinical experience includes work with adolescents, adults, Inuit, and those who violate sexual boundaries. His previous conference presentations and research publications are on the topics of self-esteem, narcissism, and professional boundaries.

Ruth E. Mann, M.Sc., C.Psychol., is Head of Sex Offender and Domestic Violence treatment programmes in Her Majesty's Prison Service (England and Wales). She has been working with sex offenders for fifteen years, and is presently responsible for the design, development and implementation of a treatment programme that treats over 1000 sex offenders per year. Roleplay is an integral part of this programme, and many of the procedures described in this book have been carefully trialled and evaluated over the last ten years.

Heather M. Moulden, BA (H), graduated with a BA (Hons) in Psychology from Queen's University in 2000 and she is currently pursuing her doctorate in Clinical Psychology at the University of Ottawa. She has been providing treatment to sexual offenders in the Canadian correctional system for the past three years. In addition to her clinical work, Heather has numerous publications and presentations. Her research interests include social intelligence, the influence of mood state, and pre-treatment benefits in sexual offender treatment.

Liam Marshall, BA(H), graduated with a B.A. (Honours) in 2000 from, and is currently a graduate student in Psychology at, Queen's University in Kingston, Ontario, Canada. Liam is the graduate student representative on the Queen's University Psychology Department Ethics and Headship committees. He is also the primary therapist of the Sexual Offender Treatment Program located at Millhaven Assessment Unit (a high-security federal penitentiary induction centre). In addition to his clinical work, Liam is an active researcher with a number of presentations at international conferences and publications, including two book chapters. Liam's sexual offender research interests include the influence of temporary mood states, elderly sexual offenders, attachment issues, and excessive sexual desire disorder.

W. B. Marshall, is an Emeritus Professor of Psychology and Psychiatry at Queen's University in Canada and the Director of Rockwood Psychological Services which provides treatment for incarcerated sexual offenders. He has been treating and doing work with sexual offenders for 34 years and has over 250 publications including 9 books. Bill was the 1999 recipient of the Santiago Grisolia Prize for his worldwide contributions to the reduction of violence and in 2000 he was elected a Fellow of the Royal Society of Canada. Bill is currently the Past-President of the Association for the Treatment of Sexual Abusers (ATSA).

Geris Serran, BA(H), is currently completing her doctoral degree in clinical psychology at the University of Ottawa. She is also employed at Rockwood Psychological Services where she works as a sexual offender therapist at Bath Institution, a medium security facility. Her research interests include therapeutic process, coping strategies, and treatment of sexual offenders. She has authored several chapters, journal articles and presentations at international conferences in these domains.